BRADSHAW'S GUIDE TO BRUNEL'S RAILWAYS

Volume Two: Swindon to South Wales

John Christopher

AMBERLEY PUBLISHING

Right: One of the many incidents of Victorian railway travel depicted by *Punch*:

The Branch Station
Miss Tremmles (who is nervous about railways generally, and especially since the late outrages). 'Oh, porter, put me into a carraige where there are ladies, or respectable people, or ...'
Porter. 'Oh, you're all safe this mornin' miss; you're th' only passenger in the whol' tr'ine, except another old woman.'

About this book

This book is intended to encourage the reader to explore many aspects of the railway journey from Swindon to Pembrokeshire and the branches to Ross and Monmouth. Through Bradshaw's account and the supportive images and information it describes the history of the line, its engineering works, architecture and some of the many changes that have occurred over the years. Hopefully it will encourage you to delve a little deeper when exploring Brunel's railways and other works, but please note that public access and photography is sometimes restricted for reasons of safety and security.

First published 2014

Amberley Publishing
The Hill, Stroud
Gloucestershire, GL5 4EP

www.amberley-books.com

Copyright © John Christopher , 2014

The right of John Christopher
to be identified as the Author of this work
has been asserted in accordance with the
Copyrights, Designs and Patents Act 1988.

ISBN 978 1 4456 2177 7
EBook 978 1 4456 2192 0

British Library Cataloguing in Publication Data.
A catalogue record for this book is available from the British Library.

Typeset in 9.5pt on 12pt Celeste.
Typesetting by Amberley Publishing.
Printed in the UK.

Bradshaw on Brunel

The stupendous iron Railway Bridge by which the line is carried over the river Wye, is one of the most remarkable in the country. Bridges of this size are so rare that we think it right to direct the attention of the reader to this one. Mr Stephenson's magnificent Britannia Bridge displays one method of crossing wide spans. The Chepstow bridge of Mr. Brunel is another mode, and shows, as might have been expected, his peculiarly original and bold conception, accompanied by extraordinary economy, by arranging his materials in the form of a large suspended truss, and attaching the roadway to suspended chains kept in a state of rigidity by vertical trusses or struts, inserted between the chains and a circular wrought iron tube, spanning the river, 309 feet in length.

Bradshaw's description of the tubular railway bridge at Chepstow is interesting for several reasons. Most notably, because he refers to 'Mr' Brunel by name.

This is the second volume in the Amberley series of books based on *Bradshaw's Descriptive Railway Hand-Book of Great Britain and Ireland* which was originally published in 1863. Our first volume covered the journey from Paddington all the way to Penzance in Cornwall. For the entire length of this journey on the Swindon to South Wales line Brunel was also responsible as engineer for the Cheltenham & Great Western Railway as well as the South Wales Railway, both of which were absorbed within the Great Western Railway. In addition to the mainline, several

Isambard Kingdon Brunel
Two images of the engineer: An engraving by Mayall based on a studio photograph. *Inset*: This statue in Swindon is a copy of the Marochetti one on the Embankment in London. That tall column could represent either a locomotive's chimney stack or even an exaggerated version of Brunel's stovepipe hat.

of the branches, going to Hereford, Ross, Monmouth and Cheltenham, are also included later on.

Bradshaw's guide is aimed at the general traveller and is not written from an engineering perspective. Having said that, Bradshaw was right on the button in identifying Brunel's strongest characteristics, saying that the Chepstow bridge shows 'his peculiarly original and bold conception'. Nobody can argue with that. It is just a shame that British Railways weren't listening when they had the ageing and weakened Chepstow bridge dismantled in the 1960s. *See pages 30–31.*

Bradshaw and Brunel

George Bradshaw and Isambard Kingdom Brunel were close contemporaries who both enjoyed considerable success in their chosen fields and died while relatively young. Bradshaw, born in 1801, died in 1853 at the age of fifty-two, while Brunel who was born just a few years later in 1806 was fifty-three years-old when he died in 1859.

In all likelihood the two men never met, but their names were drawn together by an unprecedented transport revolution which took place during their brief lifetimes. It was Brunel and his fellow engineers who drove the railways, with their cuttings, embankments and tunnels, through a predominantly rural landscape to lay the foundations of the nineteenth century industrial powerhouse that has shaped the way we live today. It is fair to say that the railways are the Victorians' greatest legacy to the twentieth and twenty-first centuries. They shrank space and time. Before their coming different parts of the country had existed in local time based on the position of the sun, with Bristol, for example, running ten minutes behind London. The Great Western Railway changed all that in 1840, when it applied synchronised railway time throughout its area. The presence of the railways defined the shape and development of many of our towns and cities, they altered the distribution of the population and forever changed the fundamental patterns of our lives. For many millions of Britons the daily business of where they live and work, and how they travel between the two, is defined by the network of iron rails laid down nearly two centuries ago by Brunel, his contemporaries and an anonymous army of railway navvies.

The timing of the publication of Bradshaw's guidebooks is interesting. This particular account is taken from the 1863 edition of the handbook although, for practical reasons, it must have been written slightly earlier, probably between 1860 and 1862. By this stage the railways had lost their pioneering status, and with the heady days of the railway mania of the 1840s over they were settling into the daily business of transporting people and goods. By the early 1860s the GWR's mainline from London to Bristol, for example, had been in operation for around twenty-years and was still largely in its original as-built form. It was also by this time that rail travel had become sufficiently commonplace to create a market for Bradshaw's guides.

As a young man George Bradshaw had been apprenticed to an engraver in Manchester in 1820, and after a spell in Belfast he returned to Manchester to set up his own business as an engraver and printer specialising principally in maps. In

George Bradshaw

As with Brunel, George Bradshaw's fame and prosperity grew with the rapid spread of the railways. Although the two men were close contemporaries – they were born and also died only a few years apart – there is no record of them having met. Having previously ignored Brunel's Royal Albert Bridge at Saltash – *Vol 1 Paddington to Penzance* – Bradshaw makes up for it this time when writing about the tubular bridge at Chepstow. *See page 30.*

Inset left: A nineteenth-century Great Western Railway coach and, *below*, the twentieth century version in distinctive cream and brown livery. This is one of two coaches located at the superb Tintern station site and now used as a Tourist Information Centre and gift shop. *See page 28.*

THE FIRST "BRADSHAW"

A reminiscence of Whitsun Holidays in Ancient Egypt. From an old-time tabl(e)ature

Above: Punch's take on the ubiquitous Bradshaw guides and timetables.

October 1839, he produced the world's first compilation of railway timetables. Entitled *Bradshaw's Railway Time Tables and Assistant to Railway Travelling* the slender cloth-bound volume sold for sixpence. By 1840 the title had changed to *Bradshaw's Railway Companion* and the price doubled to one shilling. It then evolved into a monthly publication with the price reduced to the original and more affordable sixpence.

Although George Bradshaw died in 1853, the company continued to produce the monthly guides and in 1863 it launched Bradshaw's *Descriptive Railway Hand-Book of Great Britain and Ireland* (which forms the basis of this series of books). It was originally published in four sections as proper guidebooks without any of the timetable information of the monthly publications. Universally referred to simply as 'Bradshaw's Guide' it was this guidebook that features in Michael Portillo's *Great British Railway Journeys,* and as a result of its exposure to a new audience the book found itself catapulted into the best-seller list almost 150 years after it was originally published.

Without a doubt the Bradshaw Guides were invaluable in their time and they provide the modern-day reader with a fascinating insight into the mid-Victorian rail traveller's experience. In 1865 *Punch* had praised Bradshaw's publications, stating that 'seldom has the gigantic intellect of man been employed upon a work of greater utility'. Having said that, the usual facsimile editions available nowadays don't make especially easy reading with their columns of close-set type. There are scarcely any illustrations for a start, and attempts to trace linear journeys from A to B are interrupted by distracting branch line diversions. That's where this volume comes into its own. *Bradshaw's Guide to Brunel's Railways, Volume 2,* takes the reader on a continuous journey from Swindon via Gloucester all the way to Pembrokeshire. The locations of Bradshaw's diversions on to the branch line routes are indicated in the text in square brackets, but for the most part these have been grouped in a

Above: Great Western, a broad gauge loco of the Iron Duke class, built in 1846.

final section in order to maintain the flow of our main journey. The illustrations show scenes from Victorian times and they are juxtaposed with new photographs of the locations as they are today. The accompanying information provides greater background detail on Brunel, his railways and the many locations along the route.

The railways

Although the map showing the railway network covering the South West and Wales was published by the GWR in the 1920s, various parts of the railways were originally built and operated by a number of independent companies. Thus the journey might begin in Swindon, the engineering hub of the GWR, the main part is on other lines which only later became subsumed within the GWR. However, as we shall see, almost all of them have close Brunel connections and most were constructed to his broad gauge which is why they are included.

The journey begins with the line up from Wiltshire, through the Sapperton Tunnel into the Golden Valley and on to Stroud and Gloucester; a line which was initiated by the Cheltenham & Great Western Union Railway (C&GWUR). This had been authorised by Parliament in 1836 with Brunel as engineer, although much of the work was carried out by one of his assistants, Charles Richardson. However, when the C&GWUR ran out of money it was sold to the GWR in 1845. To the east of Stroud the line passed through Stonehouse and then curved upwards to join the Bristol to Gloucester line. This was another of Brunel's railways and opened in 1844 – it merged with the non-Brunel Birmingham & Gloucester Railway two years later to form the short-lived Birmingham & Bristol Railway, which, in turn became part of the Midland Railway in 1846 and which shared the line coming up from Bristol with the GWR.

From Gloucester the trains into southern Wales rode on the South Wales Railway (SWR) – linking with the Gloucester & Dean Forest Railway at Grange Court – going as far as Neyland, initially. Its primary purpose was to transport coal out of Wales, but Brunel saw it as a way to connect with the transatlantic liners going to New York as well as with the ferries to Ireland. The section on the

8

far side of the River Wye, between Chesptow and Swansea, opened in June 1850, and the link with the Gloucester end was achieved in 1852 when the Chepstow bridge was completed. Trains were operated by the GWR under a lease agreement until the SWR amalgamated with the GWR in 1862.

Four further lines are covered in the final section of this book and for the most part they were broad gauge branches. The first was to Cheltenham on the Birmingham & Gloucester's mixed-gauge line which opened in 1840, although at one time the town had three stations serving the GWR and the Midland Railway. The next line is the Hereford Ross & Gloucester Railway (HR&GR). This opened in 1851 as a broad gauge line and was amalgamated with the GWR in 1862. The third is the Monmouthshire line which branches from the Gloucester to Newport line to go up the Wye Valley to Ross, where it connected with the HR&GR. The final line is the Taff Vale Railway which opened in 1836 and remained independent until 1922. Brunel was engineer to the line but selected the rival 4 feet 8¼ gauge to suit the windings of the River Taff. In addition to these, the broad gauge Neath Vale Railway which connected the docks at Swansea with Merthyr Tydfil, via Aberdare, is included within the Cardiff to Newport section.

One final note: If you are wondering why Bradshaw makes no mention of the lines to Cardigan or Aberystwyth, it is because these had not been completed by the time the *Hand-Book* was published. The Aberystwyth & West Coast Railway, built as standard gauge, only opened to Aberystwyth in 1864, while the Carmarthen & Cardigan Railway, which was broad gauge initially, ran into financial difficulties and was not completed until much later, in 1895.

Below: Westbound HST 125 at Kemble Station in Gloucestershire.

Swindon

This small Wiltshire town became the engineering hub of the GWR on a site selected by Brunel and Gooch. *Left:* An early broad gauge locomotive on the central transverser in the Repairing Shop. Designed by Brunel, this 290-foot wooden building was demolished in the 1920s to make way for new workshops.

Above: An early view of Swindon Junction. Note the very tall totem signal. Located halfway between Bristol and London, this was the junction for the Cheltenham & Great Western Union Railway which went northwest via Cirencester and Stroud to join up with the Bristol & Gloucester Railway at Standish to the west of Stonehouse. Both of these broad gauge lines were later absorbed within the GWR network, as shown in this company map from the 1920s.

Swindon to Gloucester

SWINDON JUNCTION

Distance from station, 1 mile.

A telegraph station.

Refreshment rooms at the station.

MARKET DAY – Monday.

FAIRS – Monday before April 5th, second Mondays after May 12th and September 11th, second Mondays before October 10th and December 12th.

MAILS – Two arrivals and departures, daily, between London and Swindon.

MONEY ORDER OFFICE.

BANKERS – County of Gloucester Banking Co.; North Wilts Banking Co.

SWINDON, on the Great Western, like Wolverhampton and Crewe on the North Western, is one of the extraordinary products of the railway enterprise of the present age. It is a colony of engineers and handicraft men. The company manufacture their own engines at the factory, where cleaning and everything connected with constructive repair is carried on.

The refreshment room at this station is admirably conducted, and abundantly supplied with every article of fare to tempt the best as well as the most delicate appetites, and the prices are moderate, considering the extortions to which travellers are occasionally exposed.

The valley of **Stroud** through which the railway passes from Swindon to Gloucester, is well known to travellers and tourists as presenting a continuous series of lovely landscapes. The valley is almost in the character of a mountain gorge, with a branching stream in the bottom, which partially furnishes the motive power for the numerous cloth and fulling mills of the district, the quality of the water, too, being peculiarly adapted for dyeing purposes.

Swindon to Cirencester, Stroud, Gloucester, and Cheltenham.

PURTON.

Distance from station, 2 miles.

A telegraph station.

MAILS – One arrival and departure, daily, between London and Purton.

The next station is MINETY, soon after leaving, we enter

GLOUCESTERSHIRE

One of the western counties, which presents three beautiful varieties of landscape scenery, viz: the hill, vale, and forest. The hill district, including those of Cotswold and Stroudwater, may be considered as a continuation of the central chain proceeding

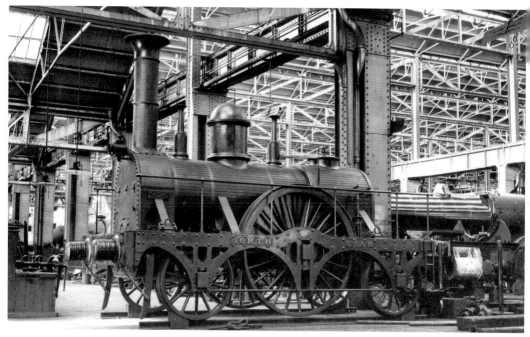

Swindon Works and village

Above: After the demise of the broad gauge two locomotives were stored at the GWR Works in Swindon. Alas, both of these, *Lord of the Isles* and *North Star* were later scrapped in 1906 to free up space. This replica of *North Star* was built in 1923 using some original parts including the driving wheels.

Left: It's dinner time at the Swindon Works, as depicted by this postcard *c.* 1905. The Works closed in 1986 and although many of the workshops were demolished some parts have survived including the imposing frontage of the main entrance.

Opposite: The erecting shop photographed in 1927.

In addition to the GWR Works at Swindon the 'village' grew up to house the railway workers and meet their needs with shops, pubs and the Mechanics Institute – paid for by subscription – which was a mixture of library and sports/arts/health centre. The cottages, built between 1841 and 1865, were designed by Brunel in collaboration with Matthew Digby Wyatt who had also worked on Paddington station. The former 'barracks' building, *shown right*, was used by the GWR museum for a time and is now a performance venue.

Kemble

The station seen from the road bridge, with the truncated branch to Cirencester Town on the right. Today Kemble is an important stop for train services to Paddington and caters for an affluent catchment area including Tetbury and Cirencester. The station in Cirencester closed in 1964 and the old station building is in the middle of a car park with the Waitrose supermarket occupying the site of the former goods yard.

Above and left:
The Sapperton Tunnel takes the railway line through a ridge of the Cotswolds to emerge at the top of the Golden Valley. The tunnel is in two sections and the southern portal of the main one can be seen on the north side of the main Tetbury to Cirencester road. The ventilation shaft is in the woods nearby. Note the brickwork added above the stone blocks.

south from Derbyshire, and passing through this county into Wiltshire, there expanding into the Salisbury downs, and afterwards running in a western direction towards Land's End in Cornwall. The downs, which formerly lay open, producing little else than furze, are now converted into arable enclosed fields, and communications have been opened between towns, where formerly the roads were impassable.

That part of the county called the vale district, is bounded on the east by the Cotswold hills, and the river Severn on the west; it is usually subdivided into the vales of Evesham, Gloucester, and Berkeley. The characteristic features of the entire district are nearly the same; though if a difference be admitted, it will probably be in favour of that of Berkeley.

The vale of Evesham follows the Avon eastward to Stratford, and in respect to climate, produce, etc., resembles that of Gloucestershire, which in its outline is somewhat semicircular, the river Severn being the chord, and the surrounding hills the arch; the towns of Gloucester, Tewkesbury, and Cheltenham, forming a triangle within its area.

The vale of Berkeley, called the Lower, is of a more irregular surface than the upper one. The scenery is in general very beautiful. The forest district is separated from the rest of the county by the river Severn; and principally contains the Forest of Dean, which was celebrated for its fine oaks. Lead and iron ores exist in abundance. Coal is also very plentiful.

At a distance of 6 ½ miles beyond Minety, the train stops at

TETBURY ROAD (TETBURY)

Population of the parish, 3,274; the station itself is near to the little village of Kemble.

Distance from station, 7 miles.

A telegraph station.

HOTELS – Talbot; White Hart.

MARKET DAY – Wednesday.

FAIRS – Ash Wednesday, Wednesday before and after April 5th, July 22nd.

BANKERS – County of Gloucester Bank.

CIRENCESTER – (BRANCH).

Distance from the station, ¼ mile.

A telegraph station.

HOTELS – The King's Head; Ram.

MARKET DAYS – Monday and Friday.

FAIRS – Easter Tuesday, July 18th; Monday before and after Oct. 11th; Nov. 8th.

BANKERS – County of Glo'ster Banking Co.; Brank of Glo'stershire Banking Co.

Distances of places from the station

	Miles		Miles
Barnsley Park	5	Lypiatt Park	8
Beggar's Down	6	Malmesbury	8
Bownham House	8	Misserden Park	7

The Golden Valley

Heading towards Stroud, the first station reached after emerging from the Sapperton Tunnel is at Chalford, *shown top left.* However, this was a later addition to the line and was opened in 1897. Chalford later became the main stabling point for the GWR railmotors which operated through the valley. The bridge for the Cirencester road is on the left of the station in this postcard view looking westwards down the valley.

"HOLMES GAVE ME A SKETCH OF THE EVENTS."

Middle left: Bradshaw describes the valley as 'presenting a continuous series of lovely landscapes ... almost in the character of a mountain gorge'. Another pair of distinguished travellers to come this way, albeit a fictional duo, were Sherlock Holmes and his companion Dr John Watson in the short story, *The Boscombe Valley Mystery.* Watson describes passing through the 'beautiful Stroud valley' on their way to Ross-on-Wye.

Left: The little signal box at the St Mary's Crossing, between Chalford and Brimscombe, is post-Brunellian but a charming survivor nonetheless. GWR boundary markers, mounted on short lengths of broad gauge rail, can be found beside the nearby canal path.

Cherrington Grove	7	Northleach	10
Cirencester Abbey	0 ½	Penbury Park	4
Down House	3 ½	Rendcomb Park	5
Edgeworth	5 ½	Rendon Park	5
Foss Cross	6	Sapperton Park	3
Hill House	4	Stroud	

Cirencester is one of the greatest marts in England for wool. The magnificence of the church in this place entitles it to rank amongst the first in the kingdom. Here three Roman roads meet, and from the variety of Roman coins, tessellated pavement, and other antiquities found in the neighbourhood, it seems to have covered a much wider area than at present.

Cirencester was formerly fortified, and the ruins of the walls and streets may still be seen in the adjacent meadows.

Swindon to Gloucester line continues.

BRIMSCOMBE
A telegraph station.
HOTEL – Railway.
MONEY ORDER OFFICE at Stroud.

STROUD
POPULATION, 35,517.
A telegraph station
HOTELS – George; Lamb.
MAILS – Two arrivals and departures, daily, between London and Stroud.
MARKET DAY – Friday
FAIRS – May 12th and August 21st.

Stroud is a market town, situated near the confluence of the river Frome and the Slade Water. Woollen cloth forms the staple manufacture of the town and its environs. Returns two members to Parliament.

Distances of places from the station

	Miles		Miles
Bownham House	2	Misserden Park	5
Creed Place	6¼	Nimpsfield	4
Easington	4½	Painswick	3
Frodmore	2	Penbury Park	6
Haresfield	4½	Quedgeley House	6
Hill House	5	Rodborough	1
Hock's House	6	Rudge	2¾
Horns, The	1	Stancomb Cross	3
Hyde Court	3	Standish House	4½

Into Stroud

The line through the Golden Valley makes a number of crossings over roads, canal and river, and consequently it featured nine of Brunel's viaducts. They were of timber originally, although all of these had been replaced with brick by the early 1890s. This is the combined Capel and Canal viaduct beside the A419.

Above: Brunel's Stroud station looking westwards with GWR railmotor No. 6. It was an important station on the C&GWUR, which opened in May 1845. The tall chimney is part of the now demolished Watts brewery. *(Image Archive)*

Right: The surviving broad gauge goods shed on the north side of the tracks at Stroud. A fine building, it has been preserved and is now used as a venue by a local arts group. This photograph was taken in 2005 before steel shutters were added to the railway entrances.

King's Stanley	3	Tuffley Court	5
*Lypiatt Park	2	Whitcomb Park	6
Minchinhampton	3	Woodchester	2

STONEHOUSE

Distance from station, ½ mile.

A telegraph station.

HOTELS – Crown and Anchor; Plough.

At this point the line joins the Bristol and Birmingham rail, which proceeds on the left to Bristol, and on the right to Gloucester and Cheltenham.

GLOUCESTER

POPULATION, 16,512.

A telegraph station.

HOTELS – King's Head, W. Churchill; first-class Family and Commercial, highly recommended as a most comfortable house, in the centre of the town. Bell and Wellington.

MARKET DAYS – Wednesday and Saturday.

FAIRS – April 5th, July 5th, Sept. 28th, and Nov. 28th.

BANKERS – County of Glo'ster Banking Co.; Glo'stershire Banking Co.; National Provincial Bank of England; Thomas Turner.

A cathedral city, capital of the county, and parliamentary borough (two members), on the Severn, and the Bristol and Birmingham Railway, 114 miles from London, in a flat spot, which was under water in the floods of 1853. At Kingsholme, to the north, on the site of a Roman station, called *Glevum*, the later Saxon kings had a seat, which, Canute attempting to take, was defeated, in the battle of Alney Island, close by. Laxington and other pleasant hills overlook the vale of Gloucester, a rich loamy tract of 60,000 acres, where considerable corn, fruit, beans, turnips, and hay are raised, though much of the butter and double Gloucester cheese, for which the county is noted, comes from the Wiltshire meadows. The corn market is held every third Monday, from July to November.

This town is situated on an eminence, in that division of Gloucester called the vale, near the banks of the Severn, and when viewed from that river it presents a very imposing appearance. The city possesses many elegant public buildings, and a magnificent cathedral, which is particularly celebrated for its architectural beauty. The *Cathedral* is a cross, 426 feet long; the oldest parts are the Norman crypt and nave, built in 1089. The later English choir is the work of Abbot Wigmore (about 1330), and a 'whispering' passage, 75 feet long, near the fine east window, which is 79 feet long by 35 broad, or one of the largest in England. The west front was built in 1437; the tower, which is 225 feet high, was begun a little later, but not finished till 1518; the Lady Chapel, 92 feet long, is the most modern part. There is a very old tomb of Edward II, (who was murdered at Berkeley Castle), also monuments of Robert Curthose the Conquerer's brother, and *Dr. Jenner*, the discoverer of vaccination. Some of the Lacy family are buried in the Chapter House. The beautiful cloisters

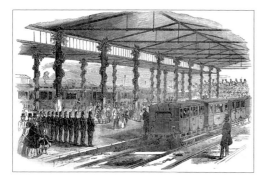

Gloucester

Top left: Queen Victoria at Gloucester station in 1849. As this image from *The Illustrated London News* shows, even Royalty had to change trains at Gloucester where Brunel's fine broad gauge met the narrower so-called 'standard' gauge rails. Consequently, Gloucester became the rallying cry for the anti-broad brigade. *See page 94.*

Left: The view along Southgate Street in Gloucester, *c.* 1890. *(LoC)*

Left and below: Gloucester docks with the Cathedral in the background. The Cathedral dates back to the seventh century and is the resting place of King Edward II who was murdered at Berkeley Castle. Another resident of Berkeley was Edward Jenner, the pioneer of the smallpox vaccine. Although buried at the family grave in Berkeley this memorial statue is at the Cathedral. *(Wendy Harris)* The caracturist James Gillray mocked Jenner's use of the cowpox agent in his vaccine by depicting its recipients growing cow horns. Jenner is shown standing, wearing the brown coat. *(LoC)*

The Cow Pock — or — the Wonderful Effects of the New Inoculation! — vide the Publications of ye Anti-Vaccine Society

were built between 1351 and 1392. Of the twelve churches, those of St. Catherine and St. Mary de Lode are Norman in part, and St. Nicholas is early English. At St. John's is a tablet to the Rev. T. Stock, who with *Raikes* established the 'four original *Sunday Schools* in this parish and St. Catherine's, in 1780.' From this small beginning sprung that gratuitous system of Christian instruction which has covered the face of England and Wales with schools. Gloucester boasts another evangelist in *Whitfield*, who was born at the Bell Inn, while Bishop Hooper, whom it enlisted in the noble army of martyrs, was burnt in St. Mary's Square. Close to the rail and the ship canal basin is the County Gaol (on the castle site), where the separate system was first tried, 1790. Shipping come up to this basic by a cut from the Severn, near Berkeley; there is a good import trade. In this part also are the *Spa Gardens* and pump room, over a mineral spring of some value. The Shire Hall was built by Smirke; the Infirmary covers a space of seven and a half acres. In Commercial Street is a *Museum,* the gift of the Guises of Elmore Court. Pins are made here.

In the environs are the gate of Lanthoney Abbey, *Highnam Court*, seat of T. G. Parry, Esq., in the renaissance style; Churchdown, a solitary hill, having the Cots Wolds to the right, from 800 to 1100 feet high; Cheltenham and its mineral waters; Hempstead Harwick, Painswick, and other seats; Newent old priory; *Flaxley Abbey*, seat of Sir M. Boevey, Bart; the Forest of Dean, an interesting hilly wooded tract, stretching to the Wye, and producing iron, coal, stone, etc.; Ross, and its spire, built by Kyrle, the 'man of Ross,' overlooking the Wye, the beautiful scenery of which may be visited from here, as well as the Malvern hills, with the Hydropathic establishments of Drs. Wilson and Gully. *Goodrich Court*, seat of the Meyricks, near Ross, which has a remarkable collection of armour, etc., and is near a fine old Norman castle of the Pentroches.

Distances of places from the station

	Miles		Miles
Badgworth	3	Longford	1½
Barnwood	0½	Maizmore	3
Brookworth	3	Quedgeley	3
Churchdown	2½	Rudford	1
Elmore Court	5	Sandhurst	3
Forton	3	Studgrive	2
Hatfield Court	5	Upton	3
High Grove	3	Whaddon	3
Highnam Park	4	Wooten	1

[Cheltenham on the Gloucester to Birmingham line – *see page 71*]

Bullo Pill

The little creek at Bullo Pill, on the north shore of the Severn, was connected via the Forest of Dean railways to the mines in the area. At its height, the Bullo Pill Railway was handling up to 1,000 tons of coal, iron and stone a day. The bridge carries the South Wales line over the entrance to Bullo Pill.

Left: In 1868 the GWR's *Rob Royal* was derailed at Bullo Pill after running into the back of a cattle train from Carmarthen. This photograph of the aftermath seems to show a competition to see who could climb the highest. Note the variety of dress and headgear denoting the role of the various railwaymen. The top-hatted figure is clearly the most senior. *(National Archives)*

Right: One of the two signal boxes at Lydney. This is the Lydney Crossing box on the mainline to South Wales, while the other is for Lydney Junction where the former Severn & Wye branch heads northwest into the Forest and now forms part of the Dean Forest Railway heritage line.

This 1920s GWR map shows the line passing under the Severn through the tunnel, *see overleaf,* but before the tunnel was completed the trains from Swindon had to take the longer route going via Gloucester and down the far side of the estuary.

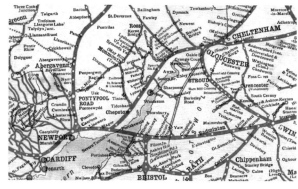

Gloucester to Newport

South Wales Railway

Gloucester to Newport

This line of railway affords great facilities to tourists and lovers of the picturesque for visiting the beautiful scenery of Wales.

Gloucester is not the central point of communication between the north and the south, the east and the west of the kingdom. From Plymouth there is an uninterrupted run though Bristol and Gloucester into the farthest points of the north where the iron road has yet pierced its way.

Upon starting, the line proceeds over an embankment and viaduct over the low meadows near the Severn, and then passes over the two bridges, and continues along the west bank of the Severn. The beautiful spire of Higham new church appears in view, and is quickly left behind, and in a few minutes the train reaches the first station on the line, which is called 'Oakle Street,' a rural spot, convenient for Churcham.

Grange Court Juction – Westbury-upon-Sever, 1 mile distant. The trains of the Hereford, Ross, and Gloucester Railway turn off at this station to the right.

[Gloucester to Hereford branch line – see page 73]

Grange Court To Newport

The forest hills are soon approached, and then we obtain a glimpse of the Severn, and passing on through Broadoak, we reach the station at

NEWNHAM
> Situate in a cutting.
> Telegraph station at Glocuester, 10½ miles,
> HOTEL – Bear
> MARKET DAY – Friday
> FAIR DAYS – June 11th and October 18th.

Newnham stands on an eminence rising from the western bank of the Severn, which is here nearly a mile across at high water. In the Norman times, it appears to have been a fortified town, designed to repress the incursions of the Welsh. The houses are principally ranged in one long street, and the church stands on a cliff, near the river.

Immediately after leaving this station a short tunnel passes underneath the East Dean Road, and emerging thence, a fine reach of the Severn, called Bullo Pill, is presented to view.

The line passes along the margin of the river for several miles, and in some

Crossing the Severn

Brunel was engineer to the Bristol & South Wales Union Railway which ran off GWR lines north of Temple Meads to a pier at New Passage. Here passengers caught a ferry to Portskewett and the junction of the South Wales Railway. Opened in 1863, after Brunel's death, in theory it offered a considerable saving on the journey via Gloucester. The Severn Railway Bridge, *below*, was not completed until 1879. *(CMcC)*

THE SEVERN BRIDGE FROM THE VIADUCT. WP. 35.

Above: The Severn Railway Bridge seen from the eastern side where it crossed over the canal to the north of Sharpness. Two spans of the bridge collapsed in 1960 after it was hit by barges in dense fog. *(CMcC)*

Right: The Severn Railway Tunnel was completed in 1886 after a very difficult build. The tunnel remains as the major rail link with South Wales.

Chepstow

On the western side of the River Wye we enter Monmouthshire and the old market town of Chepstow. Famed for its imposing castle, this Photochrom image from *c.* 1890 shows the less familar view of Chepstow looking across the town itself. The 1863 *Bradshaw* comments that the town has 'within the last few years been much improved.' *(LoC)*

Above: Whether you enter Cheptow by rail or on the A48 road bridge, you can't fail to be impressed by the Castle ruins overlooking the Wye. Construction commenced in Norman times. It fell into disuse as a garrison in the late seventeenth century and within a hundred years it had become a 'picturesque' ruin. It is now a tourist attraction under the care of Cadw, the body with responsibility for historic sites within Wales. *(LoC)*
Right: The High Street. *(CMcC)*

places the water is so near, that at high tides it approaches close to the railway.

GATCOMBE station (Purton).

LYDNEY

At the distance of 5½ miles from this station is *Clearwell Castle*, the seat of the Dowager Countess of Dunraven.

The railway here crosses the rivers Severn and Wye.

WOOLASTON

Distance from station, 4 miles.

Telegraph station at Chepstow, 5½ miles.

MONEY ORDER OFFICE at Chepstow.

We here leave the county of Gloucester, and enter that of

MONMOUTH

A small English county, bordering on the principality of Wales, which, in point of fertility, picturesque scenery, and historic remains, is the most interesting district, in proportion to its size, of any in the kingdom. The general aspect of this county is inviting, both from its diversity and fertility. A continual recurrence of hill and dale, wood and water, corn fields and meadows; the sublimity of wildly magnificent, and the beauty of mild and cultivated scenery, combine to delight the eye of the beholder at every turn he takes in this district. Nor is the air less congenial to health than the face of the country is interesting to view. The river Wye, which runs through this county, is celebrated for its picturesque scenery. The peculiar characteristic of this beautiful river are its sinuous course, the uniformity of its breadth, and the variegated scenery on its banks. So considerable is its serpentine course, that the distance from Ross to Chepstow, which is not seventeen miles in a direct line, is by water forty-three. The effects of this sinuosity are numerous, diversified, and striking; and they principally arise from two circumstances, the mazy course of the river, and the loftiness of its banks. In consequence of this, the views it exhibits are of the most beautiful kind of perspective. From the constant shifting of the foreground and side screens, the same objects are seen from a variety of sides, and in different points of view.

CHEPSTOW

POPULATION, 3,364

Distance from station, ¼ mile.

A telegraph station.

HOTEL – Beaufort Arms.

FLYS etc. – Fare to Tintern Abbey and back, time not exceeding eight hours, carriage and pair for seven persons, 16s.; driver and gates 6s.; for ten persons, 20s. and 6s. Fly for two persons, 8s. and 3s. 6d. per mile. Single horse, 1s.

MARKET DAYS – Wednesday and Saturday, and last Monday in each month.

FAIRS – Monday before March 1st, Whit Friday, June 22nd, August 1st, Friday on or before Oct. 29th.

Tintern

Dominating this part of the Wye valley, the dramatic 'stone skeleton' of Tintern Abbey. It never fails to impress visitors as they come around the bend in the road. 'The building suddenly bursts upon you ... its huge gables tanding out against the sky with a mournful air of dilapidation.' *Top right:* Seen from across the river, *c.* 1890. *(LoC)*

Right: The preserved signal box and the old railway station building at Tintern, on the route of the Wye Valley Railway which opened in 1876. The station closed for passenger trains in 1959 and for freight traffic in 1964 when the line itself closed. Now owned by the local council, it has been refurbished as a cafe and visitor centre, the latter housed in two railway carriages – *see page 6.* This section of former railway line is now part of the Wye Valley Walk.

Bottom right: A GWR boundary marker at the old station, Tintern.

Chepstow is a market town, in the county of Monmouth, situated near the mouth of the river Wye. The town is large and has within the last few years been much improved. It was formerly surrounded by walls, and defended by a castle.

Excursionists visit Tintern Abbey, Wyndcliffe, and Chepstow Castle, which are thus described in Mr. Cliffe's *Guide Book of South Wales*:

Tintern Abbey – The graceful Wye, filled up to its banks, and brimming over with the tide from the Severn Sea, glides tranquilly past the orchards and fat glebe of 'Holy Tynterne.' On every side stands an amphitheatre of rocks, nodding with hazel, ash, birch, and yew, and thrusting out from the tangled underwood high pointed crags, as it were, for ages the silent witness of that ancient Abbey and its fortunes; but removed just such a distance as to leave a fair plain in the bend of the river, for one of the most rare and magnificent structures in the whole range of ecclesiastical architecture. As you descend the road from Chepstow, the building suddenly bursts upon you, like a gigantic stone skeleton; its huge gables standing out against the sky with a mournful air of dilapidation. There is a stain upon the walls, which bespeaks a weather-beaten antiquity; and the ivy comes creeping out of the bare, sightless windows; the wild flowers and mosses cluster upon the mullions and dripstones, as if they were seeking to fill up the unglazed void with nature's own colours. The door is opened – how beautiful the long and pillared nave – what a sweep of graceful arches, how noble the proportions, the breadth, the length, and the height.

The Castle is a noble and massive relic of feudalism; the boldness of its site, on a rick overhanging the river, the vastness of its proportions, render it a peculiarly impressive ruin. The entrance is a fine specimen of Norman military architecture: the chapel is one of the most elegant structures ever built within a house of defence. It was originally founded almost immediately after the Conquest.

The **Wyndcliffe** rises in the background of the view, from the road out of Chepstow to Monmouth. Having ascended the crag, the eye ranges over portions of nine counties, yet there seems to be no confusion in the prospect; the proportions of the landscape, which unfolds itself in regular, yet not in monotonous succession, are perfect; there is nothing to offend the most exact critic in picturesque scenery. The 'German Prince,' who published a tour in England in 1826, and who has written the best description of the extraordinary view which Wyndcliffe commands – a view superior to that from Ehrenbreitshtein on the Rhine – well remarks that a vast group of views of distinct and opposite character here seem to blend and unite in one!

The stupendous iron Railway Bridge by which the line is carried over the river Wye, is one of the most remarkable in the country. Bridges of this size are so rare that we think it right to direct the attention of the reader to this one. Mr. Stephenson's magnificent Britannia bridge displays one method of crossing wide spans. The Chepstow bridge of Mr. Brunel is another mode, and shows, as might have been expected, his peculiarly original and bold conception, accompanied by extraordinary economy, by arranging his materials in the form of a large suspended truss, and attaching the roadway to suspended chains kept in a state of rigidity by

Brunel's Chepstow Bridge
Above: Two views of the bridge across the Wye at Chepstow; an especially awkward site with cliffs on one side and marshy ground on the other. At Chepstow, Brunel experimented with the use of tubular girders, a design that led directly to the Royal Albert Bridge at Saltash. *Left:* Bradshaw also mentions Stephenson's tubular bridge across the Menai Straits which used rectangular iron tubes to contain the rails. *(CMcC)*

By the 1950s the bridge had become too weak to deal with the increasingly heavy trains. It was dismantled in 1962 and replaced by an underslung girder bridge. Apart from the iron columns, only fragments have survived, such as the section of rail deck, *above left*, which is now at Brunel University in Uxbridge, London. The A48 road bridge, completed in 1988, runs parallel to the railway bridge and provides the perfect platform for a close-up view of the rail deck.

Wye Valley

The River Wye is the fifth-longest in the UK. The deep and winding valley on the section between Chepstow and Monmouth is known for its dramatic limestone gorge.

Left: The cliffs overlooking the river at Symonds Yat, on the edge of the Forest of Dean, are popular with rock climbers. These are the Seven Sisters rocks.

The Wye Valley Railway was a standard gauge line running up the Wye Valley from Chepstow, through Tintern and up to Monmouth. Following the valley bottom it crossed over the river, linking England and Wales, at several points. This striking viaduct at Penallt is a reminder of the scale of the undertaking. It is no longer in use by the railway, but a pedestrian crossing has been added on the northern side of the viaduct to connect the villages of Redbrook and Panallt. This footbridge provides a great close-up view of the viaduct.

vertical trusses or struts, inserted between the chains and a circular wrought iron tube, spanning the river, 309 feet in length. The railway having to cross a rapid and navigable river without interruption to vessels, the Admiralty very properly required that the span over the mid channel should not be less than 300 feet; and that a clear headway of 50 feet above the highest known tide should be given. The bridge is 600 feet long; there are three spans over the land of 100 feet each, which are supported upon cast iron cylinders, six feet in diameter, and one and a quarter inch thick. These were sunk to an average depth of 48 feet through numerous beds of clay, quicksand, marl, etc., to the solid limestone rock, which was found to dip at an angle of forty-five degrees; it had therefore to be carefully levelled horizontally, and the cylinders bedded level. These were then sunk by excavating them within, and pressing them down with heavy weights, in doing which very great difficulties were overcome – immense volumes of fresh water were tapped, requiring a thirty-horse engine to pump them out. They were, when finally filled with concrete, composed of Portland Cement, sand, and gravel, which is set in a few days, as hard as a rock. The concrete is filled up to the level of the roadway, so that, should the cylinder decay, it might be taken out and replaced in sections in safety.

There are six cylinders at the west end of the main span; upon those a standard, or tower of cast iron plates, 50 feet high, is erected. A similar tower of masonry is built at the east end, on the rocky precipice of the Wye.

On the west standard is a cross girder of wrought iron, and upon which the tubes rest. The tubes serve to keep apart and steady the towers; and to their ends are attached the suspending chains. Now, in an ordinary suspension bridge, the chains hang in a festoon, and are free to move according to the limited weights passing under them; but this flexibility would be inadmissible in a railway bridge, and the continuity of the bridge would be destroyed if a very small deflection took place when passed over by a heavy locomotive. With a view to give the necessary rigidity, Mr. Brunel introduced at every third part a stiff wrought iron girder, connecting firmly the tube to the roadway girders; and, with the aid of other adjusting screws, the suspension chains are pulled or stretched as nearly straight as possible. Other diagonal chains connect these points, so that at whatever part of the bridge an engine may be passing, its weight is distributed all over the tube and chains by these arrangements. The tube is strengthened within by the introduction of diaphragms or discs at every 30 feet, which render it both light and stiff. The bridge cost £65,420; and required 1,231 tons of wrought, and 1,003 tons of cast iron. The bridge has been visited by a great number of engineers from all countries; indeed, it is only by a personal inspection that the numerous ingenious contrivances and arrangements can be understood. The whole seems to be very simple, yet engineers fully enter into the complexity of the design, and the minute and carefully proportioned scantlings given to every past. We would especially call their attention to the cast iron ring or circle attached to the ends of the tube to prevent collapse; to the wedges introduced under the vertical trusses to adjust the exact tension upon the chain; to the curve given to the tubes themselves, increasing their strength; and to the rolling-boxes under the vertical trusses, by which means the road girders are maintained in a position to

Newport's transpoter bridge, *right,* is one of three surviving examples in the UK. They were built over waterways where it was important to provide adequate clearance for high-masted ships. The others are at Middlesbrough and Warrington. The Newport bridge was built in 1906.

Newport Docks

At the dawn of the industrial age this small fishing town at the mouth of the River Usk was transformed into one of the biggest docks in the country. These were mainly used for the movement of coal as well as iron and steel from the South Wales foundries. During the 1960s the Cashmore's breakers yard at Newport scrapped many of the redundant steam locomotives. *(CMcC)*

expand or contract, independently of the movements of the main tubes.

Scenery of the Wye – The Wye rises in the Plinlimmon Mountains, in the heart of South Wales, and winds along the borders of several counties, past Builth, Hay, Hereford, Ross, Monmouth, to the Bristol Channel, below Chepstow; a course of 130 miles, through scenes of great beauty and celebrity. The *Upper Wye* reaches down to Hay, on the borders of Herefordshire; after which, that portion which crosses the county is rather tame; but at Ross the *Lower Wye* begins, and ends at Chepstow. 'The former (says Mr. Cliffe, in his *Book of South Wales*) has not been estimated as it deserves, because it is off the beaten track; but the opening of the railroads to Hereford (in 1853) has brought the charming scenery of the *Upper Wye* within easy reach.' It is a rapid stream, occasionally swollen by deep floods, running between high rocky banks all the way.

From *Llangurig*, which is ten miles from its source, the river rushes through deep glens and ravines, past the junction of the Dernol, and the Nanerth cliffs (three miles long) to *Rhayader-Gwy*, i.e., the Falls of the Gwy (the Welsh name of this river), so called from a cascade made by the river, close to the bridge. It stands among mountains, and has some fragments of a castle. Within a few miles is Llyn Gwyn, in which croaking trout are caught. Hence to Builth is fourteen miles. The Elan, Clarwen, and Ithon join before you reach Builth, the last at Pont-ar-Ithon, a fine spot. The Ithon may be ascended to *Llandrindod Spa*, where there are excellent saline sulphur, and iron springs, in a healthy, though unattractive spot, with a pump-house.

Builth, is a fine part of the river, has remains of a castle, and a long bridge. Trout and salmon fishing; fine scenery. Just above it, the *Irvon* joins; it should be ascended for its charming scenery to *Llanwrtyd Wells* (fourteen miles) and *Llandovery* (twenty-three miles). When Llewellyn was hemmed in by the English under Mortimer, in Edward I's reign, he tried to get assistance to disguise his

Below: Commercial Street, Newport. *(CMcC)*

35

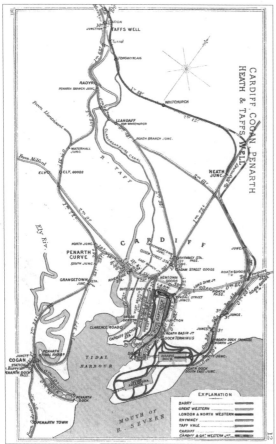

Above: This paddle steamer was one of several operated by the P&A Campbell company. In their heyday during the inter-war years they provided pleasure cruises down the Bristol Channel as well as regular crossings, running between Cardiff to Bristol and Weston-super-Mare. *(CMcC)*

Left: Railway chart from 1911 showing the tangle of lines into the busy Cardiff, Cogan and Penarth docks – the main shipping points for the huge quantities of coal coming from the South Wales coalfields.

Below: Lines of coal trucks at the Penarth docks with the 'tippler' towers used to load the coal onto colliers.

movements from the Welsh garrison of Builth Castle. It was in winter, and he had his horse's shoes reversed; this, however, was revealed to the English by the blacksmith. The garrison refused to help him, and as he was retreating up the Ithon, he was surprised and killed. *Bradwyr Buallt* is the designation applied to Builth to this day. The Welsh prince was killed at Cwm-Llewellyn, near the Park Wells; and the body buried at Cefn-y-bedd, a mile or two further on the Llandovery road. There are two roads down the Wye from Builth, the highest road being on the west side; but the east road is the most interesting, especially about Aberedw, which lies in a beautiful defile, where the Ebw falls in, opposite Erwood. The castle was Llewellyn's hunting seat. Near it is the church on a cliff, a hole in which is Llewellyn's cave. Further on the Machwy (Little Wye) joins; it should be followed a little way to the Pwll Dwu or Black Rock, and its waterfall, 40 feet down. Then comes *Llangoed Castle* (J. Macmamara, Esq.), on the Brecon side, and *Boughrood* (an old castle), on the Radnor side, which commanded the old ford here. Brecon is eight miles from this, and from that place the fine scenery of the Usk may be descended. The Hatterel, or Cradle mountains, to the right are 2545 feet high.

Glasbury, fifteen miles from Builth. Three Cocks, a good inn. *Gwyrnefed* is Colonel Wood's seat. W. Wilkins took the name of De Winton nearly twenty years ago, and *Maeslwch Castle* is the property of Captain De Winton.

Hay, four miles from here, is an old Norman town, founded by Bernard Newmarch; part of the castle remains, which was destroyed by Owen Glyndwr. It is exactly on the borders of three counties. Here the Upper Wye scenery ends. Barges are able to reach this point. *Clifford Castle,* three miles from Hay, was the birthplace of Fair Rosamund Clifford. It was built by the Conqueror's kinsman, Fitz-Osbourne.

PORTSKEWET, MAGOR, and LLANWERN stations.

NEWPORT
A telegraph station.
HOTEL – King's Head; West Gate.
MARKET DAYS – Wednesday and Saturday.
FAIRS – 14 days before Holy Thursday, August 15th, Nov. 6th, Holy Thursday.

This is a sea port town of some importance, having a population of 23,249. It has a constant steam packet communication with Bristol and various parts of South Wales; and by means of its ready access by railway with the many iron districts in the neighbourhood, its traffic in that mineral, as well as coal, of late years has greatly increased. With the exception of the church, which presents various styles of architecture, the town itself has no prepossessing attractions. The scenery from the church-yard is very imposing, taking in, as it does, a wide expanse of country, as well as an extensive view of the Severn. Outside the town a stone bridge of five arches crosses the river Usk. It was erected at a cost of something over £10,000.

[Newport to Monmouthshire line – *see page 79*]

Cardiff
The medieval castle was much admired by the Victorians and during the nineteenth century the castle and mansion were remodelled in a Gothic revival style. Cardiff Castle is now run as a tourist attraction and many events have been held in its grounds including military tattoos and musical performances. A new interpretation centre opened in 2008. *(LoC)*

Above: An 1844 print showing the view southwards across the town with the tall masts of the ships in the dock visible beyond the roof tops.

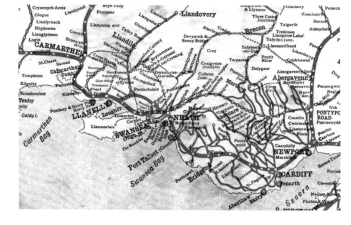

Right: GWR map of the railway network, published in the 1920s.

Cardiff to Camarthen

South Wales continued

Newport to Cardiff

From Newport, we pass through a short tunnel and cross the river Ebw, soon after arriving at

Marshfield Station, situated in a dreary extent of country, called the Westloeg Level. Crossing the river Rumney, we enter

GLAMORGANSHIRE

One of the most southern counties in Wales, by far the largest and most beautiful in the principality, and generally considered the garden of Wales.

The mountains are not so high as those in many of the surrounding counties, but their extreme abruptness imparts an air of wildness and elevation which greatly exceeds the reality. But what principally distinguishes this county is the profusion of coal, iron, and lime-stone, with which is everywhere abounds. These mineral riches have raised Glamorganshire to great importance during the last half century. Immense establishments have been erected in the wildest part of the country; canals and roads have been formed, at great expense, to connect them with the coast; and these circumstances, reacting over the whole district, and even far beyond it, have spread the influence of improvement throughout – the facilities of intercourse creating new sources of industry.

CARDIFF

POPULATION, 32,954.

A telegraph station.

HOTELS – Cardiff Arms, Angel.

MARKET DAY – Saturday.

FAIRS – Second Wednesday in March, April, and May, June 29th, September 19th, and November 30th.

Cardiff, a borough town, and capital of Glamorganshire, is built on the east bank of the river Taff or Tay, near its entrance into the mouth of the Severn. The inhabitants carry on a considerable trade with Bristol, and export a great quantity of wrought iron and coal to foreign parts.

The new Bute Docks, made on a tract of waste land, by the Marquis of Bute, who is lord of the manor, are about one mile below the town, deep enough for ships, with a basin of one and a half acres, and an entrance 45 feet wide. A ship canal 1400 yards long, 67 yards wide, runs up to the town. The coal and iron of Merthyr Tydvil and the neighbourhood are the chief exports, and the quantity

Cardiff Central Station
The largest and busiest station in South Wales, and the eleventh busiest in the UK outside of London, also happens to be an extremely fine example of Art Deco architecture. Built of silvery grey Portland stone, between 1932–1934, its wide frontage bears the Great Western Railway name with a sense of permanence that has long outlined the company itself. Initially called Cardiff Station, it became Cardiff General in 1924 and then Cardiff Central in 1973. The airy booking hall is lit by an array of angular Art Deco lamps, and the signage on the stairwells and passageways leading to the platforms is picked out in relief tiling. While the station building might not be of Bradshaw's vintage, it would not look out of place as the backdrop in one of Hercule Poirot's adventures. In 2014 work is due to begin on a £200m regeneration scheme to increase train capacity in Cardiff and the surrounding area.

almost doubles itself every two or three years.

There are remains of the town walls, with the Norman keep, 75 feet high, of the *Castle,* in which Robert Curthose (i.e., short legs), did in 1133, he having been imprisoned there for life by his brother, Henry I. The parish church is very old, and has a good tower. The new *Town Hall,* just built by H. Jones, is a handsome Italian pile, 175 feet long, including a police court, judges' and other rooms, and a *nisi prius* court. There is also a large county gaol.

Within a short distance are – *Hensol,* which belonged to Lord Chancellor Talbot; and *Wenvoe Castle,* the seat of R. Jenner, Esq., with a front of 374 feet.

[Cardiff branch on Taff Vale line – see page 87]

Cardiff To Neath

Our onward progress from Cardiff brings us through Ely, St. Fagans, and Peterston, to

LLANTRISSANT
POPULATION, 5,492
Distance from station, 1 ½ mile.
Telegraph station at Bridgend, 9 miles.

At a distance of eight and a half miles is the market town of *Cowbridge* and its ancient well-endowed grammar school; and five miles beyond is situated *Froumon Castle,* the seat of Oliver Jones, Esq.: it belonged to the St. Johns of Bletsoe, and Colonel Jones, the regicide, and contains a beautiful portrait of Cromwell.

PENCOED station

Below: Postcard, *c.* 1910, with a general view of Cardiff looking south. *(CMcC)*

BRITISH COAL STRIKE - IDLE DOCK LABORERS, CARDIFF

Cardiff Docks
A rare photograph of dock workers at Cardiff, in this instance taken during the coal strike of 1910. (LoC)

Left: The Commercial Dry Dock. Owned by the GWR this was the largest dry dock in the port of Cardiff at the time this photograph was taken in the 1930s. It shows the 15-ton electric crane handling the propeller of the *Marita*, a Norwegian ship.

BRIDGEND

A telegraph station

HOTELS – Wyndham Arms; Railway.

MARKET DAY – Saturday.

BANKERS – Sub Branch of National Provincial Bank of England.

Five miles from this improving town, at which the county elections are held, lies situated, on the coast, *Dunraven Castle* (anciently called Dindryfan, and the residence of Caractacus), the beautiful and romantic seat of the Dowager Countess of Dunraven, the heiress of the late Thomas Wyndham, Esq., who represented the county of Glamorgan in parliament for upwards of forty years.

PYLE station.

PORT TALBOT

A telegraph station.

HOTELS – Talbot Arms, and Railway.

MONEY ORDER OFFICES at Neath.

Three miles distant is *Margam Park*, the seat of C.R.M. Talbot, Esq., M.P., the descendant of the Mansells. Here is an orangery, 327 feet by 81, which contains the produce of a cargo from Holland, intended for Queen Mary, but wrecked here in 1694. A bay tree, 60 feet high, and 45 in diameter, spread, and a magnificent forest of oak trees, for which the Government in 1800 offered £40,000.

BRITON FERRY station.

Below left: Traditional Welsh costume. *(LoC) Right:* Opening of the Swansea & Neath Railway with the first train passing Neath Abbey Station.

The Landore Viaduct

Brunel used timber extensively for the construction of bridges and viaducts at a time when strong Baltic pine was readily available. The viaduct at Landore, near Swansea, was the longest of these wooden structures and had a central span of 100 feet. A similar design was also used at Newport.

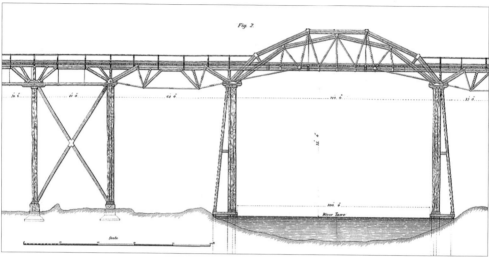

Swansea Station

Built by the South Wales Railway, later amalgamated with the GWR, the station at Swansea opened in 1850. It wasn't originally on the mainline and until 1879 passengers connecting to London or Fishguard had to change at Landore two miles to the north. The present frontage was completed in 1934, and is shown in a GWR publicity photograph from that time, *lower left*. For most of its existance the station was known as Swansea High Street, and following the closure of Swansea Victoria in the 1960s this was shortened to Swansea. The modern bilingual Welsh/English signage says Abertawe/Swansea.

NEATH

POPULATION, 6,810.

A telegraph station.

HOTEL – Castle.

MARKET DAY – Wednesday.

FAIRS – Last Wednesday in March, Trinity Thursday, July 31st, September 12th, and last Wednesday in October.

Neath, is a coal and mining port, with an ancient castle, and some abbey ruins. Here the fine Vale of Neath may be ascended to the beautiful waterfalls at its summit *(see Merthyr Tydvil, page 89)*.

VALE OF NEATH RAILWAY

Neath to Merthyr

From Neath we again turn out of our course, and pass the stations of Aberdylais, Resolven, and Glyn Neath. From this point, *Craig-y-linn,* the highest mountain in Glamorganshire, with its lakes and ravines, and which here makes a bold horse-shoe sweep, raising its huge bulk against the sky, may be reached.

HIRWAIN, junction of line to Aberdare, LLYDCOED, and ABERNANT stations follow, arriving at

MERTHYR TYDVIL.

South Wales Continued.

Neath To Llanelly.

Llansamlet station

LANDORE (SWANSEA JUNCTION)

Here passengers change carriages for Swansea, two miles distant. The view they obtain here of the valley down to Swansea is very striking. If at night, the lurid glare from countless coke ovens – if by day, the dense clouds proceeding from hundreds of chimney stalks overhanging the valley, and at all times, the arsenical sulphurous vapour filling the air, and which you may both smell and taste, give the scene a character scarcely to be seen elsewhere.

SWANSEA

A telegraph station.

HOTELS – Mackworth Arms, and Castle.

Races in September. Regatta in July.

MARKET DAYS – Wednesday and Saturday.

FAIRS – Second Saturday in May, August 15th, October 8th, July 2nd, second Saturday after October 8th.

Swansea railways
The Rhondda &
Swansea Bay Railway
connected the
coal mines of the
Rhondda valley with
the Swansea Bay
ports.

Top left: On 29
November 1865 a
train of the Vale
of Neath Railway
plunged from a
box girder bridge
at Swansea's North
Dock. The driver and
stoker were killed in
the accident.
Middle left: It is hard
to imagine anyone
offering a jigsaw of a
dock nowadays. This
magnificent wooden
jigsaw shows
the new docks at
Swansea. Produced
by the Chad Valley
company for the
GWR in 1924.
(CMcC)
Bottom left:
Swansea Docks is
the collective name
for several docks to
the east of the city
centre. Like many
of the big docks,
Swansea had its own
stable of shunters.
This is a Swansea
Harbour Trust 0-4-0T.
(CMcC)

BANKERS – Branch Bank of England; Branch of Glamorgan Banking Co.; and West of England.

This important seat of the *copper trade*, is also a parliamentary borough (one member), jointly with Neath, etc., and stands at the head of a fine bay, on the west side of *Glamorganshire*, 216 miles from London, by the Great Western and South Wales Railways, population, 41,606. No copper ore is found in this part of Wales, but coal being abundant, it is brought hither from Cornwall and foreign countries to be fluxed. For this purpose, six-sided calcines, 17 to 19 feet long, and oval furnaces, 11 feet long, are used in the copper works, of which eight are here, on the river Pauley, or by the sea-side; one employing 500 to 600 men. The earliest was established about 1720, after the Cornish tinners began to take notice of copper, which hitherto they had thrown away. The ore or shiff goes through various processes, such as calcining and melting, calcining the coarse metal, which leaves about one-third copper; then melting this to fine metal, leaving three-fifths or more than half copper; calcining the fine metal; melting the same to pigs of coarse copper, which gives nine-tenths pure metal; and lastly, roasting for blistered copper and refining it into cakes for use, which are 18 inches by 12. In this way a yearly average of 20,000 tons of copper are smelted here, from the ore brought not only from Cornwall, but from America and Australia, valued at about one and a half million sterling.

Swansea being at the mouth of the Tawe or Towey, is called Abertawe or *Abertowy* by the Welsh. By running out two piers into the bay, one being 18,000 feet long, a good harbour has been enclosed, but it is dry at low water; and floating docks are constructed. About 18,000 tons of shipping belong to this port. A castle was built here by the Normans, of which a massive quadrangular tower remains, and presents an object of some beauty. Beneath it is the Post Office, a building in

Below: Tram 51 is the only vehicle to be seen in Oxford Street, Swansea. *(CMcC)*

Swansea Bay

Two romanticised views of the bay, including Mumbles Rock with its lighthouse, shown *above*. The two-tier lighthouse was completed in 1794, and is still in use with solar panels powering the lantern and emegency monitoring equipment.
Below: The GWR Ocean Express, a double-header racing through South Wales with passengers from the Cunard ships at Fishguard. *(CMcC)*

the medieval style, recently erected. A large Market House, built in 1830, is 320 feet long. There are three churches, but the only one deserving notice is the parish church of St. Mary, which was rebuilt in the last century. Some of the numerous chapels are well built. The public Assembly Rooms and Infirmary are handsome edifices. The *Royal Institution of South Wales* was established in 1835, and contains an important library of works relating to Welsh history, with a museum of coal, fossils, antiquities, etc. This was the headquarters of the British Association at their visit in 1854. Besides works for copper smelting, there are others for tin, zinc, pottery, etc.; all fostered by the abundance of coal and lime raised in the neighbourhood. Anthracite coal, chiefly for steamers, abounds here, and was used by the whole of the British steam fleet reviewed in the Solent by Her Majesty Queen Victoria, on April 23rd, 1856. Gower, the poet, and Beau Nash were born at Swansea. The river Towey runs up the vale to the Black Mountains at its head, parallel to the canal. *Skelly Park* is the seat of Sir J. Morris, Bart. *Penllergur*, J. Llewellyn, Esq. Several other seats overlook the west side of the bay, and the fine sandy beach, two or three miles long, terminating at Oystermouth, a pretty little bathing place, with an old Norman castle, near the Light or Mumbles Head. Hence the county runs out in a peninsula, much resembling in size, shape, and character, that in the south west of Milford Haven. *Gower* is the name, or *Gwyr* in Welsh, signifying crooked; it is a mass or rugged limestone, traversed by a red sandstone ridge, which is 584 feet high, at *Cefn Bryn*, where there is a cromlech called Arthur's Stone. At the Conquest it was settled by various Norman knights, and the Flemings and Somersetshire men in their train. Round the castles they built at Swansea, Penrice, Ruich, Rhosili, and Loughor, their descendants are distinct from the aborigines to this day. There are similar in the county of Wexford. The poet Gower's family were natives of this part. Druid stones, old castles, and encampments, frequently occur in this country. The cliffs and caves along the coast deserve attention; while the Worm's Head, at the west extremity, near Rhosili Bay, is a scene of awful grandeur in bad weather. It is so called from the shape of the cliffs which run out three quarters of a mile long, dipping and rising like a great sea serpent (or worm). Under the very extremity, which is 200 or 300 feet high, there is a vast funnel cave. The scenery of Swansea Bay is so beautiful that it is universally styled by both natives and tourists, 'The Bay of Naples in miniature.' Aberafon or Port Talbot, a bustling mining town, near which is *Margam Abbey*, the seat of C.R.M. Talbot, Esq., M.P., beautifully wooded, and remarkable for its orangery and gardens. There are remains of an abbey of the 12th century. Further on are Ogmore and Dunraven Castles, etc.

Gower Road (Mumbles) and Loughor stations.

Leaving the Loughor Station, we cross by a low bridge the Loughor river, and enter

CARMARTHENSHIRE

Which is mountainous and woody. The air is mild and salubrious, and the whole county is remarkably healthy and fertile. Coal and limestone are found in great abundance.

Left: The swing bridge at Carmarthen, together with a diagram of the operating gear on the lifting span. These images come from the GWR's 1935 publication, *Track Topics.*

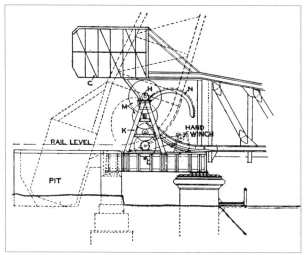

Below: No. 4 *Kidwelly* was an 0-6-0 tank built in 1903 by the Avonside Engine Company for the Burry Port & Gwendraeth Valley Railway. It later passed into British Railways ownership in 1948 and was withdrawn in 1953. Bury Port is a small town five miles from Llanelli in Carmarthenshire. *(CMcC)*

LLANELLY

POPULATION, 11,446.

Distance from station, ½ mile.

A telegraph station

HOTELS – Falcon; Ship and Castle; and Thomas Arms.

MARKET DAY – Saturday.

FAIRS – Holy Thursday, July 29th, September 30th, and November 10th.

LLANELLY RAILWAY AND DOCKS

Llanelly to Llandilo and Llandovery

Again turning to the right from Llanelly, we pass through Dock, Bynea, Llangennech, Pontardulais, and Pantyffynon.

CROSS INN and GARNANT stations, on a short branch to the right.

LLANDEBIE, DERWYDD ROAD, and FAIRFACH STATIONS.

LLANDILO

A telegraph station.

HOTEL – Cawdor Arms.

MARKET DAY – Saturday.

FAIRS – Feb. 20th, May 6th, every Tuesday, from May 14th to June 21st, Monday before Easter, August 23rd, Sept. 28th, Nov. 12th and 22nd, and Monday before Dec. 25th.

Talley Road and Glanrhyd stations.

LLANGADOCK

A telegraph station.

MARKET DAY – Thursday.

FAIRS – January 16th; March 12th; May, last Thursday; June 9th; September 1st; Thursday after the 11th; December 11th.

POPULATION – 2,189; many engaged in the production of limestone and coal, which prevail in this district.

Lampeter Road station.

LLANDOVERY

POPULATION, 1,855.

A telegraph station.

MARKET DAYS – Wednesday and Saturday.

FAIRS – January 1st, Wednesday after the 17th; March 19th; Whit-Tuesday; July 13th; October, Wednesday after the 10th; November 26th.

This straggling little town is surrounded by hills, which to the northward begin to assume a very wild and barren aspect. Here are the remains of a castle, destroyed by Cromwell.

South Wales Main Line Continued.
Llanelly to Milford Haven.

PEMBREY.
> POPULATION, 4,145.
> Telegraph station at Llanelly, 4 miles.
> MARKET DAY – Saturday.

KIDWELLY
> Telegraph station at Llanelly, 9 miles.
> HOTEL – Pelican.
> MARKET DAY – Saturday
> FAIRS – May 24th, August 1st, and Oct. 29th.

This is a small decayed borough, having a population of about 1652, engaged principally as tin workers – it has also a very limited export trade. *Kidwelly Castle* is here situated: it is reported to have been erected by William de Landres, a Norman adventurer, who conquered Glamorganshire about the year 1094. It now belongs to the Earl of Cawdor. The gateway is good, and altogether presents

Kidwelly and Carmarthen
Above: The castle at Kidwelly. Bradshaw describes it as 'a small decayed borough'.
Above right: The view towards Carmarthen looking across the River Towey valley. *(LoC)*
Right: From 1852, a contemporary engraving of the opening of the South Wales Railway at Carmarthen Junction Station, on the mainline from Swansea to Neyland. Although the station buildings are shown in the illustration, they had not been completed by the opening date.

a noble relic of ancient magnificence. Here King John took refuge whilst at war with the barons.

Ferryside Station.

CARMARTHEN

A telegraph station.

HOTELS – Ivy Bush, and Boar's Head.

MARKET DAYS – Wednesday and Saturday.

FAIRS – April 15th, June 3rd, July 10th, August 12th, Sept. 9th, Oct 9th, and Nov. 14th.

CARMARTHEN is the capital of *Carmarthenshire*, on the South Wales Railway, and the river Towey, with a population of 9,993, who, jointly with Llanelly, return one member. It is one of the most healthy towns, and commands a view of one of the finest vales in the principality. It has a good foreign and coasting trade; and boasts of a handsome town hall and market house, a Presbyterian college, free grammar school, &c &c. A column to the memory of Sir T. Picton, who represented the borough in parliament, stands on the west of the town, near the old Guildhall; also the Assembly Rooms, with a beautiful front built of freestone, in which are Reading Rooms, supported by public subscriptions. General Nott (to the memory of whom a handsome monument in bronze has been erected in Nott Square), together with Lewis Bailey, Bishop of Bangor, and author of the 'Practice of Piety,' were natives. The shire prison is on the castle site. A large *diocesan training school* for South Wales occupies 10 acres, and has a Gothic front of 200 feet long. In the old church is a monument to *Sir R. Steele*, who married Miss Scurlock, of Ty Gwyn, and died at the Ivy Bush, in King Street, to whom the Inn is reported to have belonged; the effigy of Rhys ap Thomas; with a good copy of the Transfiguration. Shipping of a small class come up to the quay; the harbour is three miles lower down, near the bay, which makes a fine semi-circular sweep, seventeen miles across. On the east side are the wild limestone cliffs of Worm's head, 300 feet high, singularly shaped, and on the other Tenby, a beautiful watering place, near the lighthouse on Caldy Island.

ST. CLEARS

Telegraph station at Carmarthen, 8½ miles.

HOTELS – Railway, and Swan.

MARKET DAY – Saturday.

FAIRS – May 4th, June 1st, Oct. 12th.

This is a mere nominal borough and market town, with a population of 1,129, engaged in the coasting and provision trade. There are the remains of a Norman castle and priory, given to All Soul's College, Oxford.

The line now leaves Carmarthen, and enters PEMBROKESHIRE.

Opening of the South Wales Railway at the Narberth Road Station in Haverfordwest. Traditional costume much in evidence. There are very few records of the costume dating before 1770 when the first tourists started coming to Wales.

Below. The first of the GWR Ocean Express special trains leaving Fishguard Station on 31 August 1909. *(CMcC)*

Right: GWR map showing the distances and routes for the Irish sailings across the St George's Channel. Fishguard to Rosslare is shown as 54 nautical miles (nm), Fishguard to Waterford 92 nm, and further south the Cork route is 140 nm, more than twice that of the crossing to Rosslare.

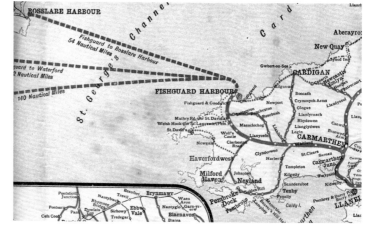

54

Pembrokeshire

The surface of this county is, generally speaking, composed of easy slopes, but not mountainous, except a ridge of hills which runs from the coast to the border of Carmarthenshire, Pembroke cannot boast of being either a trading or a manufacturing county, though it possesses many facilities for commerce. The South Wales mineral basin terminates here, and becomes shallower as it approaches the extremity. The strata are raised near the surface, and then the quality is impaired.

WHITLAND
Telegraph station at Carmarthen, 13¾ miles.
MONEY ORDER OFFICE at St. Clears.

NARBERTH ROAD (For Tenby)
    Distance of town from station, 3¾ miles.
    Telegraph station at Haverfordwest, 11¾ miles,
    HOTEL – De Rutzen Arms.
    MARKET DAY – Saturday
    FAIRS – March 21st, May 13th, June 2nd and 29th, August 10th, September 22nd, October 27th, and December 11th.

NARBERTH is a small neat town in the county of Carmarthen, with a population of 1,209. It has the privilege of being represented in parliament in connection with the borough of Haverfordwest, Fishguard, and St. Davids. It has no particular object of attraction, beyond being the best and nearest way by coach from Narberth Road station to the town of

TENBY
    POPULATION, 2,982.
    Telegraph station at New Milford, 13 miles.
    HOTELS – White Lion, and Coburg.
    MARKET DAYS – Wednesday and Saturday.
    FAIRS – May 4th Whit Tuesday, July 4th, Oct. 2nd, and Dec. 4th.
    RACES in August or September.

Tenby, on the coast of Pembrokeshire, and eleven miles from Pembroke itself, was at a very remote period occupied by the ancient Britons as a fishing town, and is most romantically situated on the eastern and southern sides of a rocky peninsula, stretching out into the Bristol Channel, and rising to the elevation of 100 feet above the level of high water. The houses are well built, and command

Milford Haven
Left: Laying the foundation stone for new Hubberston Dock within the natural harbour of the Milford Haven estuary. From *The Illustrated London News* of 27 August 1864.
Below: The docks and town viewed from Hakin which is directly to the west of Milford Haven. *(CMcC)*

MH 34   THE DOCKS AND TOWN FROM HAKIN. MILFORD HAVEN.

Left: Opening of the South Wales Extension Railway to Milford Haven in 1863.

fine views of the sea; and the beautiful situation of the town, the fine beach, and firm and smooth sands, the transparency of the sea water, and the pleasant walks and extensive drives in the vicinity, have raised it from the decline into which it had for many years previously fallen to a high rank among the most favourite watering-places on the coast. Under the Castle-hill baths, provided with every convenience, are supplied by a capacious reservoir, filled from the sea at every tide. This establishment comprises two spacious pleasure-baths, one for ladies and one for gentlemen, four smaller cold baths, and also a range of warm sea-water and vapour-baths, with apparatus for heating them to any degree of temperature required. The surrounding scenery is extremely beautiful and picturesque. The majestic masses of rock, of various forms and hues, which line the coast; the numerous bays and distant promontories that stretch out into the sea; the receding coast of Carmarthenshire, with the projecting headland of Gower enclosing the great bay of Carmarthen, on the western boundary of which the town is situated; the small islands of Caldey and Lundy, with the distant shores of Somersetshire and Devonshire, combine to impart a high degree of interest and variety to one of the finest marine expanses in the kingdom. On one side of the town there is a drive of eleven miles to the ancient town of Pembroke, through a fine campaign country, studded with churches, villages, and gentlemen's seats, surrounded with plantations and pleasure-grounds, and on the other the country is agreeably diversified with swelling eminences, clothed with verdure, and small valleys richly wooded. The remains of the ancient castle are considerable, though in a very dilapidated condition. A portion of the keep still remains, and the principal gateway, with a square tower and a bastion, are also in a tolerable state of preservation. The ancient walls, which surrounded the town, are still in many places entire. The sands afford delightful promenades, and abound also with shells of varied descriptions, not less than one-half of the British collection of 600 varieties having been found on this coast, among which have been several of value commonly esteemed foreign. The church is a venerable and spacious structure, dating as far back as the year 1250. There is constant steam communication with Bristol.

CLARBESTON ROAD

Distance from station, 3 miles.
Telegraph station at Haverfordwest, 5½ miles.
MARKET DAY – Saturday.
MONEY ORDER OFFICE at Narberth.

HAVERFORDWEST

POPULATION, 7,019.
A telegraph station.
HOTEL – Castle.
MARKET DAYS – Tuesday and Saturday.
FAIRS – March 20th, April 14th, May 12th, June 12th, July 18th, August 9th, September 4th and 23rd, October 18th, and December 10th.

Milford Haven

This is the largest natural harbour in Wales. The first rail links to Milford Haven came with the completion of the South Wales Railway in 1856. At that time, Brunel saw the estuary port at Neyland as a direct link between the railway and the steamships going to New York, and the town grew rapidly as a result. The hotel is shown *above*. Milford Haven is still a working port and has the large oil terminal offshore.
Middle left: Milford Fisheries' boat *Thomas Connolly* on the slips at Milford Haven. *(CMcC)*

Tenby Harbour

Located on the western side of Carmarthan Bay. The railway station opened in 1863. Bradshaw writes at some length on this 'romantically situated' seaside town. *(LoC)*

HAVERFORDWEST is a borough town in Pembrokeshire, South Wales. It stands on a western branch of the river Claddau, which at spring tides is navigable for vessels of a hundred tons burden, and for whose accommodation a number of convenient quays have been erected. The town is built on the steep declivity of a hill, and presents a very picturesque appearance, as the houses rise in terraces one above the other, the whole being crowned by the ruins of the castle. The interior of the town, however, is in many respects inconvenient and disagreeable, as many of the streets are so narrow and steep as almost to prevent horses and carriages from ascending them. But, on the other hand, the spirit of modern improvement has prevailed to a considerable extent, and many new streets and public buildings have been erected. There are three churches, a handsome guild hall, the gaol, and the keep of an ancient castle.

DISTANCES OF PLACES FROM THE STATION

	Miles		Miles
Abercastle	17¾	Milford	7½
Abernause	17	Pembroke Castle	11½
Benton Castle	9	Penlan Castle	17
Bishop's Palace at St. Davids	17¼	Picton Castle	4¾
Cardigan	26	Poyntz Castle	7
Carew Castle	15	Roch Castle	6
Cathedral (St. Davids)	16½	Skower and Skokam Islands	12
Cromlech	(2)	Soloa Valley	8
from Nevern Chruch	18	St. Bride's Bay	5
Devil's Punch Bowl	20	St. Davids	16
Huntersman's Leap	21	Walwin Castle	4

MILFORD ROAD
Telegraph station at Haverfordwest, 4¾ miles.

MONEY ORDER OFFICE at Haverfordwest, 5 miles.

Johnston Hill, in the vicinity, is the seat of Lord Kensington. Anthracite, or smokeless coal, abounds in this district, and it is only wanting to be better known, I order to be generally used in the steamers belonging to the naval and merchant services. It was used by Her Majesty's steam fleet at the review on the 23rd of April, 1856.

It has been proposed to construct a railway, 3½ miles long, from this station to the town of Milford; other modes of conveyance are at present in use.

MILFORD
HOTELS – Royal; Victoria.

MARKET DAYS – Tuesday and Saturday.

Robert Thomas's statue of Brunel on the quayside at Neyland. Erected in 1999, it shows him holding the *Great Eastern* steamship in one hand and a broad gauge loco in the other. In 2010 the bronze statue was stolen, most probably for its value as scrap metal. *(Frank Whittle)*

The town of Milford has a population of 3,007 partially engaged in ship-building. It is pleasantly situated; but since the removal of the royal dockyard and Irish packet station from here, about 1815, to Pater and Pembroke, on the opposite side of the Haven, its importance in a commercial point of view has much declined.

Milford is prettily situated on a sloping point of land, about six miles from the entrance of the Haven, to which it gives its name. Milford haven ought to be viewed from the water. The lower and broadest portion of the Haven runs in an easterly direction for about twelve miles, and then turns abruptly to the north, forming several reaches towards Haverfordwest. The scenery around Milford is very picturesque. On a fork of land, formed by the confluence of the two rivers Cleddy and Cleddau, stands Rose Castle, an ancient seat of the Owens, and higher up on the estuary is Picton Castle.

NEW MILFORD
A telegraph station.

This has become a station of much importance, being the one used for the interchange of traffic to and from the South of Ireland.

PEMBROKE
The capital of the county, and Pater or Pembroke Dock, the seat of a royal dockyard, at the head of that magnificent inlet called Milford Haven, opposite to Neyland station (from which it is distant one and a half mile), and the terminus of the South Wales line, opened in April, 1856. A branch is in progress to unite it with the main line and the beautiful watering place of Tenby; in conjunction with which, and two or three other little boroughs, it returns one member to parliament. Population, 15,071. Both the town and shire take their name from the Welsh words, *Pen fro*, signifying the head of the peninsula, as the town lies on a long point, marked on both sides by a creek or Milford Haven. In this commanding spot, Arnulph de Montgomery began a Norman Castle in 1092, which a few years after was strengthened by the famous Richard de Clare, or Strongbow, before he sailed for the conquest of Ireland. Its ruins still exist on a hill over the town; the round keep is 75 feet high. There is a large cave under the hall; and in one of the town-gates the Earl of Richmond (whose mother was of the Welsh family of Tudlor of Tudor, descended from Edward I.), afterwards Henry VII, was born. He landed on this part of Wales after his escape from confinement in Brittany; and supported by Rhys ap Thomas, and other Welsh adherents, marched towards Bosworth Field, where his defeat of Richard III., and subsequent marriage with Elizabeth of York, terminated forever the wars of the roses.

There is nothing else worth notice in the town, except the old church of St. Michael. Two short bridges cross to Monckton (where there was a priory), and to the suburbs on the north side, from whence roads, about two miles long, lead to Pembroke ferry and to the dockyard at *Pater*, which covers a site of 88 acres,

Brunel's *Great Eastern* steamship

Above: The *Great Eastern* in her prime. Completed in 1859 the ship had been intended for the Australia run, but instead operated out of Milford Haven, sometimes Liverpool, crossing the Atlantic to New York. Following a successful career as a transatlantic cable layer, she was laid up at Milford Haven and offered at auction in October 1885. *Below:* After a brief period as a floating showboat and advertising hoarding she was broken up at Rock Ferry on the Mersey in 1889–1890. *(CMcC)*

fifteen or sixteen of which are occupied by iron building slips. The sea front is nearly half a mile long; one new slip has an open glass and metal roof. Important docks are in progress, which will cost £100,000. The whole is defended by strong forts at Hobb's Point Jetty, formerly the station for the Waterford Mail Packets, now discontinued, near the large hotel. Until 1814 the dockyard was at Milford, five miles to the left, on the north side of the Haven, which has declined since its removal. The establishment of a packet station for New York and the south of Ireland, which is one of the chief objects contemplated by the South Wales Railway Company, may contribute to revive it. It possesses a little coasting trade. *Pill Priory* is near.

On Thorn Island, on the southern side of the entrance into Milford Haven, there are newly-erected fortifications, which are now strongly garrisoned. The noble Haven which it overlooks in in fact the mouth of the Cleddau or Cleddy, and is twelve miles long, by two miles broad, with fifteen bays or creeks in it. As there is plenty of deep water, it would easily hold the entire British navy. At the entrance is St. Anne's light. Imogen (one of the sweetest of Shakespeare's heroines), says, in 'Cymbeline,' when she receives her husband's letter:

'Oh for a horse with wings! Hear'st thou, Pisanio?
He is at *Milford Haven*. Read and tell me
How far 'tis thither. If one of mean affairs
May plod it in a week, why may not I
Glide thither in a day?
    And, by the way,

Tell me how Wales is made so happy as
To inherit such a haven!'

Here, in 'a mountainous country, with a cave,' disguised as a boy, the poor betrayed lady afterwards meets with her royal brothers Guiderus and Arviragus, supposed to be sons of the old shepherd Belarius.

'*Bel.* This youth, howe'er distressed he appears, hath had
Good ancestors.
Arv. How angel like he sings.
Gui. But his neat cookery! He cut our roots in characters;
                And sauc'd our broths, as Juno had been sick,
                And he her dieter.'

In the course of the plot, Lucius, the Roman General lands here:
After your will have coursed the sea; attending
You here at Milford Haven, with your ships.

FISHGUARD HARBOUR, S.S. "St. DAVID."

Above: The *SS St David* at Fishguard, one of the GWR's ferries operating between Fishguard and Ireland – *see map on page 54. Below:* Coastal Command Sunderland flying boats escorting the Royal Yacht *Britannia* in the 1950s. During the Second World War the Sunderlands guarded the coastal approaches. HMY *Britannia* was ordered by the Queen's father, George VI, in 1952 and built by the John Brown shipyard in Clydebank. It was commissioned in January 1954, retired in 1997 and is now a museum ship open to the public at Leth, Edinburgh. *(CMcC)*

During the troubles of Henry IV's reign, a force of 12,000 French actually landed here to support the rising of Owen Glyndwr.

The peninsula between Milford Haven and the Bristol Channel is bounded by a remarkable broken limestone coast, along which is a succession of the most striking views. When traversed from end to end, it is a walk, from Anglebay, at the Haven's mouth to Tenby, in Carmarthen bay, of twenty or twenty-five miles. Cars may be hired, but, as inns are very rare, it is advisable to take provisions, or you must trust to the chance of shelter at some hospitable farm house. Of these, however, there are but few.

Starting from the old fort near Angle or Nangle Bay, you pass round the east side of the entrance to the Haven, with St. Anne's Head and Light on the opposite side, and the island closing up to Bride's Bay, a most enchanting spot, in the distance behind. Rat and Sheep Islands are seen below, the latter near a Danish camp. The broad swell of the Atlantic dashes on the cliffs. At Gupton (seven miles from Angle fort) a little stream comes down to Freshwater Bay, from Castle Martin, an old place, noted for its breed of black hill cattle, and for a cromlech. It had a castle formerly. *Brownslade*, near it, is the seat of J. Mirehouse, Esq. At Linney Head (three miles from Gupton) the finest part of this coast trip commences. 'A greater extent of carboniferous limestone is exposed to view along these shores than in any part of Britain.' – Cliffe's *Book of South Wales*. Keep at the edge of the downs to enjoy it thoroughly. Out in the sea is the Crow rock, a dangerous one, covered at high water. The Castles are two rocks separated from the mainland. Then Flimstone chapel (a ruin); near Bull's Scaughter Bay, another group of stacks or castle rocks, swarming with razorbills, guillemots, kittiwakes, and other sea birds, in a very wild part; another camp near a dark chasm, called the Devil's Cauldron; and then *St. Gwan's Head* (seven miles from Linney Head), so called, it is said, after King Arthur's nephew, Sir Gawaine, or Gwain, of old romances. Here the cliffs are 160 or 170 feet high, and the strata in vast horizontal blocks. In a gap, looking down to the sea, is a ruined hermitage, to which you descend by about fifty-three broken steps; it is only 20 feet long. The saint's hiding place in the east wall, and his well are shown, with remnants of past superstition. *Bosherston Meer*, a little further, is a cave, which runs up the land more than quarter of a mile. The roaring of the waves and the wind along this natural tunnel is at times terrific. Before reaching it you pass a remarkable crack in the cliffs, called the Huntsman's Leap. Across Broadhaven Creek (which runs up to Bosheston) to Stackpole Head; then *Stackpole Park*, the modern seat of the Earl of Cawdor, the chief owner of the soil in this quarter. There was a Norman castle of the eleventh century here, built by a baron, whose effigy is in Cheriton church. Fine view from Windmill Hill. Round East Freshwater Bay and Swanslake Bay to *Manorbeer Castle* (eight miles from West Gwan's) close to the shore. It is a fine existing specimen of what a feudal dwelling was in early times. It was built by William de Barri, and was the birth place of Giraldus de Barri (or Cambrensis, i.e., the Welshman); Lord Milford is the present owner. Hence, round Oldcastle Head and Lidstep Point to Giltar Head (fifteen miles from Manor Bay), turning into

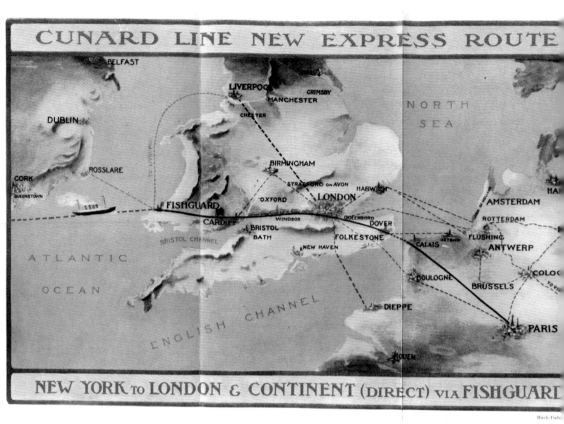

Above: Cunard Line map showing the Fishguard connections. *(CMcC)*

Carnarvon Bay. Caldy Island and its lighthouse about two miles off. About twenty miles to the E.S.E., if the weather is favourable, you may catch sight of the Worm's Head, on the other side of the bay, a most striking object. Caldy has a chapel and remains of a priory upon it, incorporated with the seat of a gentleman who is lord of the island. At *Penally*, a pretty chapel and old cross; shells and seaweeds on the shore. Old castle at Trellowyn, and mineral springs at Gumperton. Then Tenby (two or three miles from Giltar Point), a most delightful bathing place to stop at.

Up the *Cleddy* are *Lawrenny Hall*, seat of L. Phillipps, Esq., on a bold point where two creeks branch off, one to Carew, Landshipping Quay, near which the two Cleddys unite. The west Cleddy may be followed to *Boulston*, an old seat of the Wogans; and Haverfordwest. The east Cleddy, to *Picton*, Lord Milford's seat – a well wooded park, with an old Norman castle; and *Slebech*, the seat of the Baron de Rutzen. Here is an old church of the Knights Templars.

In the neighbourhood of Pembroke are the following: *Upton Castle*, seat of Rev. W. Evans, *Lamphey Court* (two miles), belongs to C. Mathias, Esq., and is close to the fine ruins of a deserted palace of the bishops of St. Davids, in a rich Gothic style; the great hall is 76 feet long. There is another by the same builder (Bishop

Gower), at the city of St. Davids, the see of which, now much despoiled, had at one time six different residences for its prelates. Its cathedral, which is cruciform, 200 feet by 120 feet, with fine tower, 127 feet, is being restored, and contains the shrine visited by Henry I. and Edward I., the road to which (16 miles from Haverfordwest) is the most execrable in the United Kingdom, but replete with scenery magnificently grand. *Carew* (four miles), is another of those old baronial seats so abundant in South Wales; it was built in Henry I.'s reign, by the ancestor of the Fitzgeralds. There are two great halls 100 feet and 80 feet long. Effigies in the church; and an old roadside cross, 14 feet high. *Orielton* (6 miles) belongs to the Owens.

There has been a Steam Packet communication opened out between this place and Ireland, of which the traveller, if he think fit, might avail himself.

The end of the line
These iron rails, relics of Brunel's ill-fated broad gauge, have been reused to create dockside barriers at Neyland, Pembrokeshire.
(Derek Webb)

Ocean Express at Fishguard

Above: Carriages of the Ocean Express at Fishguard Station. These special trains were operated by the GWR between 1908 and 1914, and only when the liners were calling at the harbour.

Left: Postcard showing the lavish interior of the Dining Saloon.

Left: On the last day of August 1909, Cunard's *Mauretania* called at Fishguard on her way to Liverpool. This gave the opportunity to drop the mails from the USA so that they would reach London much more quickly, but it also ensured that those passengers for the south of England could be at their destinations much more quickly too. Mail workers are shown unloading the mail onto the SS *Smeaton*, which operated from the harbour from 1909–1910.

(All images from the J. & C. McCutcheon collection)

Right: Smartly uniformed Post Office staff pose for a photograph at the stern of the *Smeaton* at Fishguard on 31 August 1909. Liverpool was at the time still the major transatlantic port in the UK, but Southampton would soon overtake it, making the calls at Fishguard redundant.

Mails being unloaded from the *Mauretania* onto SS *Smeaton*. The *Smeaton* began her life as a passenger tender at Plymouth, and during the First World War operated in Brest, France. Sold in 1929, it was broken up at Belfast in 1947. *Right:* A baggage tender unloading at Fishguard. *Mauretania's* sister ship *Lusitania* would also call at Fishguard in September 1909.

The Cheltenham Flyer was the name of the GWR's flagship daily express from Paddington to Cheltenham.

Passenger. "Well, you say you've put all my luggage safe, what are you waiting for?—I thought you were forbidden to take money!"

Porter. "So we is, sir. We never 'takes' it—it's 'given to us!'"

Cheltenham

Top left: A Military Fete and Flower show at Cheltenham, an unlikely combination depicted in this engraving from *The Illustrated London News.* 'Gloucestershire Rifle Volunteers in the Grand Walk at Pittville Spa.'

Left: Punch's commentary on the futility of trying to stop railway porters from asking the travelling public for tips.

Bottom left: The gardens and footbridge at Pittville Park which was opened in 1825. *(LoC)*

Opposite page: Postcard view of the Promenade Gardens, *c.* 1905.

Branch Lines

[Branch line from Gloucester]

CHELTENHAM.
POPULATION, 39,693.
A telegraph station.
HOTELS – The Plough, first class, for families and private gentlemen; the Queen's, first-class, for families and gentlemen. Commercial houses, the Fleece and the Lamb.
MARKET DAY – Thursday.
FAIRS – Second Thursday in April, 2nd Thursday in Sept., Holy Thursday, Dec. 11th and 18th.
BANKERS – Branch of Glos'stershire Banking Co.; National provisional Bank of England; County of Glo'ster Bank.

CHELTENHAM takes its name from the river Chelt, and is celebrated for its medicinal waters. It has been for the last sixty years one of the most elegant and fashionable watering places in England. The town is built on a flat marshy soil, on the borders of a rich and fertile valley, and the surrounding Leckhampton hills protect it from the cold winds. The season for drinking the waters is from May to October. The climate in winter is generally mild, though in July and August the heat is felt to be oppressive. Its surface is elevated about 165 feet above Gloucester, and the funnel shape of the valley, with a large river in its centre (the

The Promenade Gardens, Cheltenham

Above: Minotaur and Hare, a Cheltenham sculpture by Sophie Ryder. *(Arpingstone)*

Chelt, which runs through to the Severn), elicits currents of air, which ventilate the atmosphere, and contribute much to the purity and salubrity of the town.

It is a parliamentary borough (one member), situated in a charming spot under the Cotswold hills, in Gloucestershire, 7 miles from Gloucester, on the Bristol and Birmingham Railway. Most of it is modern and well-built. The assembly rooms are in High Street, ¾ mile long. A little on the one side is the *Pittville Spa* and Pump Room (built in 1824), with its Grecian portico and dome, in the midst of pleasing grounds. On the other, the promenade leads to *Montpellier Spa* and *Rotunda* pump-room, and Lansdowne Crescent. A pump-room, built in 1803, stands at the *Old Wells*, first used in 1716, and approached by an avenue of elms, an object of deserved attraction, from its extent and symmetry. There is also the Chalybeate Spa. Both contain asperient salts of soda and magnesia, with a little iodine and iron; and are of great benefit in cases of weak stomachs, liver complaints and plethora. Two are chiefly chalybeate. The peaks and gardens about the town have much picturesque beauty, and are open throughout the year for a trifling fee, besides being the scene at intervals of numerous fetes and floricultural shows.

A *Proprietary College*, in the Tudor style, was built in 1843, 240 foot long. The parish church of St. Mary is in part as old as the 11th century. Christ church and St. Peter's, among the modern ones, deserve notice – the latter being in the Norman style, with a round tower, &c.

In 1831, Mr. Gurney tried his locomotive carriages along the high road to Gloucester, running the distance in 55 minutes, several times a day.

In the neighbourhood are many good walks and points of view, viz., Battledown, Leckhampton Court, and Clerk Cloud, 1,134 feet high. Behind Leckhampton are the *Severn Springs,* one of the principal heads of the river Thames. *Southam* is the Tudor seat of Lord Ellenborough. *Boddington Manor,* J. Neale, Esq. Charlton Park, &c. &c.

HEREFORD, ROSS AND GLOUCESTER

Gloucester to Ross and Hereford.

LONGHOPE (late Hopebrook).
   Distance from station, 1 mile.
   Telegraph station at Gloucester, 11½ – Railway.
   MONEY ORDER OFFICE at Newent.

MITCHELDEAN ROAD station.

ROSS.
   Telegraph station at Hereford, 12¼ miles.
   HOTELS – Royal; King's Head.
   MARKET DAY – Thursday. FAIRS – Thursday after march 10th, Ascension Day,
   June 21st, July 20th, Thursday after October 10th, December 11th.
   BANKERS – J. W. R. Hall; Morgan & Co., Pritchards and Allaway.

Ross has a population of 3,715; is situated on a rocky elevation on the east bank
of the Wye. In the church are several monuments of the Rudhall family, one of
whom opposed Cromwell in his siege of Hereford. There is also one of Mr. J.
Kyrle, the celebrated 'man of Ross', who was interred here. From the churchyard

Below: The sixteenth century Market House at Ross-on-Wye, *c.* 1890. *(LoC)*

Hereford, Ross & Gloucester Railway

This broad gauge line opened on 1 June 1855. Running for just over twenty-two miles, it connected Hereford and Gloucester via the junction at Grange Court, and passed through Ross-on-Wye, *shown left*. The railway was amalgamated with the GWR in 1862 and it was an early candidate for conversion to the standard gauge which took place in 1869.

The station at Ross-on-Wye was located on the northern edge of the town, but after closure in 1964 for passenger traffic, and for goods the following year, the buildings were demolished to make way for an industrial estate.

The engine shed, *above*, still stands and it is a fine building. After a period as an architectural salvage yard it now serves as a garden centre. Unfortunately various awnings now block the view of the end of the shed where the locos once entered, and the view of the side of the shed is from the road. As the sign, *left*, indicates it was actually built in 1871 and therefore it is not a Brunellian structure as is sometimes claimed.

are some very beautiful views. Ross has great attractions during the summer months. *Goodrich Court*, the seat of Sir S. R. Meyrick, in the neighbourhood, is visited for its armoury. It may be seen on application.

FAWLEY station.

HOLME LACEY.
MONEY ORDER OFFICE at Hereford.

This is the ancient seat of the Scudamore family, now in the possession of Sir E. F. Scudamore Stanhope, Bart. The mansion and grounds excite much interest, having a good picture gallery, and a giant pear tree, covering a quarter of an acre. Here Pope wrote the 'Man of Ross'.

HEREFORD
A telegraph station.
HOTELS – City Arms, Green Dragon.
MARKET DAYS – Wednesday and Saturday.
FAIRS – Tuesday after Candlemas, Easter Wednesday, May 19th and 28th, July 1st, and October 20th.
BANKERS – National Provincial Bank of England; Hereford banking Co.; Matthews and Co.; Hoskins and Morgan.

The Market House in the centre of Ross-on-Wye is now a visitors centre.

Hereford Cattle

Left: Bradshaw tells us that the Hereford cattle are 'a splendid breed, white-faced with soft reddish brown coats'. Although not restricted to the county the 200 year-old breed is still a familiar site in the Herefordshire countryside. They are bred primarily for their meat.

Hereford Cathedral

On Easter Monday 1786 the cathedral suffered a catastrophic collapse when the west tower fell, leaving the whole of the west face in ruins. The restoration work commenced in 1841 and the cathedral was re-opened in 1863, the same year that the Bradshaw Guide was published. The west front was not restored until the beginning of the twentieth century. This aquatint by I. Wathan dates from 1888.
(British Library)

The cathedral's chained library used to house the Mappa Mundi, a medieval map drawn on vellum and dating to the late thirteenth century. On the map the city of Jerusalem is at its centre with the dark area of the Mediterranean tilted on its side in the lower half. Europe is shown to the bottom left with the British Isles squeezed into the edge of the map. In the 1980s the cash-strapped Diocese of Hereford proposed selling the map, but thanks to donations from the National Heritage Memorial Fund, Paul Getty and members of the public, it has been kept at Hereford and is now housed in a new library building in the Cathedral Close.

HEREFORD, the capital of Herefordshire, and a parliamentary borough, on the Shrewsbury and Hereford, Newport, Abergavenny, and Hereford, and Hereford, Ross and Gloucester lines. By rail, *via* Gloucester, the distance from London is 144¼ miles, but the distance by road is only 134, or 33 beyond Gloucester. Population, 15,585.

Hereford, as its old Saxon name explains it to be, stands at a *military Ford* on the Wye, which King Harold protected by a castle, the site of which, at castle Green, is now occupied by the Nelson Column, where an old bridge of the fifteenth century crosses the river a little higher. To this castle the barons brought Edward II's favourite, De Spenser, and executed him in 1322; and four years later the unfortunate king himself was here deprived of his crown. Parts of the town are low and old fashioned. Some remains of the old town walls are still visible. The soil without is a rich tract of meadow, orchard, and timber; and the internal trade is chiefly in agricultural produce, good cider and perry (which require a little brandy to qualify them), wool, hops and prime cattle – the last being a splendid breed, white-faced, with soft reddish brown coats. A few gloves and other leather goods are made. Salmon are caught.

The present Cathedral, lately restored, standing near the river, and dedicated to St. Mary, is the third on this site, the first one having been founded in the ninth century by King Offa, to atone for the murder of Ethelbert. It is a handsome cross, 325 feet long, begun by Bishop Herbert de Loxinga in 1079, when the Norman style prevailed, and finished by Bishop Borth in 1535, who built the beautiful north porch. The west front was spoiled by Wyatt, in restoring it after the fall of the tower above in 1786. There are two other Norman towers, and a great tower, which firmly support a tall spire. Some of the Gothic side chapels, and the monuments of Bishop Cantilupe, Bishop de Bethune, &c., deserve notice. A curious Saxon map of the world is in the library. The college of the Vicars-Choral, and the grammar school are in the cloisters; the latter was founded here in 1385.

The triennial music festivals are held in the *Shire Hall*, a handsome building, by Smirke, built in 1817. Near this is an ancient *Town Hall*, constructed of carved timber, 84 feet long, by 34 broad, of the time of James I, and resting on an open arcade, where the market is held; John Able was the builder. The county gaol, on the road to Aylestone Hill, is on the site of a priory, founded by the De Lacys; the infirmary, near the castle Green. At the opposite end of the town, past Above Eign, is the *White Cross*, built in 1347, to serve as a market for the country people when the town was ravaged by the plague. Near the bridge and the old palace is the preaching cross of the Black Friary. All Saints Church and St. Peter's are both Norman, though altered by late restorations. The tower of All Saints leans seven feet from the perpendicular. St. Martin's is a new Gothic church, in place of one ruined by the royalist party. Poor *Nell Gwynne* was born here.

In the neighbourhood are various points of interest. Up the Wye are – Belmont; Sugwas, once a country seat of the bishops; *Garnons*, Sir G. Cotterell Bart., in a fine spot, under Bishopstone Hill; *Moccas*, Sir V. Cornewall, Bart., in an immense park. *Sufton Court* (near a camp) is the seat of the Herefords, an ancient family. *Hampton Court*, the old seat of the Coningsbys, belongs to – Arkwright Esq., a

Two bridges over the River Monnow at Monmouth: *Above*, a print dated 1799 of the old Tibbs footbridge with St Mary's Church in the background. *Below*, a photograph of the fortified medieval gateway of the Minnow Bridge from around 1890. *(LoC)*

descendant of the great cotton spinner. *Foxley*, Sir R. Price, Bart., was planned by Price, who wrote the 'Essay on the Picturesque,' according to the principles laid down in that work. Leominster, a parliamentary borough, has many old timbered houses, especially one built by the architect of the Hereford Town Hall.

[Branch line from Newport]

Monmouthshire Line

The Eastern and Western Valleys Lines turn off at this point to the right, passing through districts rich in mineral products, but not of essential importance to the general tourist. The stations on the Western Line are BASSALLEG JUNCTION, TYDEE, RISCA, CROSS KEYS, CHAPEL BRIDGE, ABERCARNE, NEW BRIDGE, CRUMLIN, LLANHILLETH, ABERBEEG, CWM, VICTORIA, EBBW VALE, ABERTILLERY, and BLAINA. Those on the eastern Branch, LLANTANAM, CWMBRAN, PONTNEWYDD, PONTRHYDYRUN, PONTPOOL, PONTNEWYNNYDD, ABERSYCHAN, CWM AVON, and BLAENAVON.

Returning to Newport we now proceed by the

WEST MIDLAND

Newport to Abergavenny and Hereford.

In ten minutes after leaving Newport we reach PONTNEWYDD, and in ten minutes more, the station

Below: Completed in 1857, the Crumlin Viaduct carried the Taff Vale Extension of the Newport, Abergavenny & Hereford Railway over the River Ebbw.

Right: In 1930 this elephant, known as Lossey, was photographed having a splash about in the River Monnow at Monmouth. The local newspaper reported that she had escaped from the Mop Fair in the town. *(Andrew Helme)*

Above: The statue to the pioneer motorist and aviator Charles Rolls stands in front of the Shire Hall in Agincourt Square, Monmouth. Rolls was killed during a flying display held at Bournemouth in 1910. His family, significant landowners in the Monmouth area, had the statue erected in his memory.

Left: Postcard view of Crane Street in Pontypool, c. 1905. *(CMcC)*

PONTYPOOL ROAD.

> Distance from the town of the same name, 1 mile.
> A telegraph station.

Near is Pontypool Park, Hanbury Leigh Esq. This forms the junction with the

Taff Vale Extension.

A short line, 16 miles long, running into the Taff vale Line at Quaker's Yard. The stations on the line are PONTYPOOL, CRUMLIN, TREDEGAR, RHYMNEY JUNCTION, LLANCAICH, and QUAKER'S YARD.

Merthyr Tydvil, see page 89.

COLEFORD, MONMOUTH, USK, AND PONTYPOOL.

Pontypool Road to Monmouth.

About a mile and a half beyond Pontypool Road this line turns off; and at the distance of about 3½ miles further, we cross the river at Usk, and stop at the station of that name.

USK.

The town is situated a little to the right of the station, and is a place of great antiquity. Considerable remains of a castle where Richard III and Edward IV are reputed to have been born, are to be seen; likewise part of a priory. Fine salmon fishing.

Llangibby Castle (3 miles).

Passing LLANDENNY Station, we arrive at

RAGLAN ROAD,

Which is available for foot passengers only.

Here are the fine remains of the castle built by Sir W. Thomas in the 14th century. The Marquis of Worcester defended it for four years against the Parliamen: it is now a most picturesque ruin. It gives title of Baron Raglan to a descendant – the late Lord Fitzroy Somerset, Commander-in-Chief in the late war in the Crimea. He was military secretary to Wellington, and lost an arm at Waterloo. What is was in the 16th century we may hear from the poet Churchyard; he speaks of it as –

> A castle fine that Raglan hight – stands moted almost round,
> Made of freestone, upright, straight as line,
> Whose workmanship in Beauty doth abound.

DINGESTOW

Or Dynstow. In a barn, among beautiful orchards, may be seen the remains of Grace Dieu Abbey.

MONMOUTH.

Telegraph station at Pontypool road, 18 miles.

HOTELS – Beaufort Arms; King's Head.

MONMOUTH, the capital of Monmouthshire, is on a delightful part of the Wye, at the junction of the Monnow, a parliamentary borough, returning one member, conjointly with Newport and Usk, with an agricultural population of 5,710, which is rather on the decrease; but this will no doubt be augmented by the recent opening of the railway from Pontypool. It was the ancient Blestium, from which a Roman road, in the direction of the present one, went to Usk. There was a castle here, even in Saxon times, which afterwards became the residence of Henry IV, and here, in 1387, his famous son Henry V was born – 'Harry of Monmouth' – the immortal Prince Hal of Shakespeare.

The few remains of this castle (which belongs to the Duke of Beaufort), stand among houses on a ridge over the Monnow, to the west near the gaol, the walls being 6 to 10 feet thick. Here is shown the room in which Henry was born, and the great hall by the side of it. There is a statue of him in the Market Place.

Within a short distance of the town are the following objects of notice: The *Wye*, so celebrated for its uniform breadth, lofty cliffs, winding course, and picturesque scenery, which is perpetually changing its character. Elegant and commodious boats are kept here for the use of tourists. 'The stranger cannot do better than hire Samuel Dew, whom he will find by Monmouth Bridge. Sam is one of the steadiest and cleverest of Wye watermen, knows the river well, and is quite used to guiding those who are in search of the beautiful.' – *The Land we Live in.*

Near the junction of the Trothey, about a mile from Monmouth, is *Troy House*, an old seat of the Duke of Beaufort, with old portraits and gardens, where the marquis of Worcester gave Charles I a dish of fruit 'from Troy.' 'Truly my lord,' said the king, 'I have heard that corn grows where Troy stood, but I never thought that there had grown apricots there before.' Here is Henry's cradle (so called), and the armour he wore at Agincourt. About 6 miles down the Wye is Beacon Hill, 1,000 feet high, near Trelech Cross (three Druid stones), and below that Landogo Bigswear, Tintern Abbey, Wyndcliffe, Chepstow (17 miles by water); *Wonastow*, seat of Sir W. Pilkington, baronet, is a very old seat, which belonged to the Herberts. *Treowen*, near it, is another, but now turned into a farm house. Up the Trothey is *Llantillio House*.

A pretty road leads to Beaulieu Grove on the top, near the handsome spire church of Lantillio Crossenny, and the ruins of White Castle, a fortress built by the early Norman possessors of this county. In ascending the beautiful valley of the Monnow, there are two other castles worth notice – Skenfrith and Grosmont – the latter being under Greig Hill, near a small cross church. Most of these structures were formerly part of the Duchy of Lancaster, through John of Gaunt, but now belong, with large possessions, to the Beaufort family. From Monmouth, up the Wye, you pass Dixton Church, a pretty rustic building; then New Weir, Symond's Yat, Courtfield (where Henry V was nursed), &c, till you come to Ross. But the best plan is to descend from that place (see the *Wye*).

An excursion may be made to the *Forest of Dean*, and its interesting scenery.

You pass (taking the Coleford Road) the Buckstone, an immense Logan stone, on a hill, 56 feet round at the top, and tapering off to 3 at the bottom. Coleford Church is modern, the old one having been destroyed in the civil wars, when Lord Herbert routed some of the parliament people here. About 3 miles north-east is the Speech House, where the miners hold their meetings. To the south, in the direction of Offa's Dyke, which may still be traced, is *Clearwell Park*, the seat of the dowager Countess of Dunraven, where a great heap of Roman money was found in 1847, and St. Briaval's, with its *May Pole* and hundred court, part of a Norman castle. There are many deserted mines. The wood is cut for hoops, poles, and other purposes.

A good stone bridge across the Wye, and one the Monnow – an ancient stone building, called the Welsh Gate, with a Norman chapel (St. Thomas's) at the foot. Many of the houses are white-washed, and, as they are dispersed among gardens and orchards, the view of the town in summer is picturesque. The parish church of *St. Mary* has a tapering spire 200 feet. It was attached to a priory, of which there are remains in a private house adjoining. The handsome oriel window is called the 'study' of Geoffrey of Monmouth, but he was born in the 11th century, long before such a style was invented. He was a Welsh monk (Geoffrey ap Arthur), who turned the British Chronicles, fables and all, into rugged Latin. To him, however, we are indebted for Shalespeare's King Lear, and the Sabrina of Milton's *Comus*.

Monmouth was once famous for its woollen caps, 'the most ancient, general, warm, and profitable covering for men's heads on this island,' according to Fuller. The manufacture was afterwards transferred to Bewdley. This is, or was, a capper's chapel in the church, 'better carved and gilded than any other part of it.' Fletcher takes care to remember this.

The well-endowed free school was founded by W. Jones, who, from a poor shop-boy at this place, became a rich London merchant. Newland was his birth-place; and there, after quitting London, he showed himself under the disguise of poverty, but being told to try for relief at Monmouth, where he had been at service, he repaired hither, was kindly received, and then revealed who he was.

One of the walks is at Chippenham meadow, near the junction of the Monnow and Wye, under a grove of elms. Anchor and May Hills are good points of view. Past may Hill (across the Wye) is *Kymin Hill*, the east half of which is Gloucestershire.

West Midland Main Line
Pontypool Road to Abergavenny

Passing the station of NANTYDERRY, or Goitre, we arrive at PENPERGWM, near which is Llanover, the seat of Lord Llanover, and three miles to the right is Clytha. Proceeding along the valley of the USK, we soon arrive at:

Abergavenny
Above: Photochrom image looking across Abergavenny to Holy Mountain, *c.* 1890. *(LoC)*
Below: A surprisingly quiet Frogmore Street in the town. *(CMcC)*

ABERGAVENNY.

A telegraph station.

HOTEL – Angel.

MARKET DAY – Tuesday.

FAIRS – Third Tuesday in March, May 14th, June 24th (wool), Tuesday before July 20th, September 25th, and November 19th.

RACES in April.

This interesting old place, of 4,621 inhabitants, stands among the Monmouthshire Hills, near the Sugar Loaf, Blorenge, and other peaks, in a fine part of Usk, where the Gavenny joins it, and gives name to the town, which the Romans who had a station here, called Gobannium. It was formerly noted for its old castle and springs, founded by Hammeline de Balun at the Conquest, the former for the purpose of guarding the pass into Wales. This feudal structure afterwards came to the Nevilles, who still take title from it. A Tudor gate, from which there is a fine prospect, is the chief remain. Later still Abergavenny became celebrated for its Welsh wigs, made of goats' hair, some of which sold at 40 guineas each. Physicians also used to send patients here to drink goats' whey. But its present prosperity arises from its flannel weaving, and the valuable coal and iron works at Clydach, Blaenavon, &c., in the neighbourhood – a state of things likely to be much increased by the Newport, Abergavenny and Hereford Railway, part of the important chain which unites South Wales to Liverpool and the north of England.

The old bridge of 15 arches crosses the Usk. The church has some ancient tombs of the Beauchamps, and other possessors of the lordship. Traces of the old priory exist near it. There is also an old grammer school, and a modern Cymreidiggion Society's Hall for Welsh bardic meetings – Monmouth being essentially Welsh, though separated from the principality since Henry VIII's time. Antiquaries say that until feudal tenures were abolished by Charles II, Abergavenny castle used to give its holders their title by mere possession – like Arundel Castle, in Sussex, instead of by writ or by patent.

The views from the Sugar Loaf, which is 1,856 feet high, are magnificent. It takes three hours to ascend it. A still more beautiful prospect is enjoyed from St. Michael's old Chapel on Skyrrid Vawr. The White Castle is near the mountain. Raglan Castle, which the famous marquis of Worcester held out so stoutly against Cromwell, is also near (8 miles), on the Monmouth Road. Its machicolated gate, hall, chapel, the yellow tower, &c., are in excellent preservation, through the care of its owner, the Duke of Beaufort. Llanthony Abbey stands in a wild part of the Hhondu. The scenery of the Usk, from Abergavenny up to Brecon, is very romantic, as it winds round the black mountains, in one of the highest peaks of which it rises above Trecastle. Excellent trout fishing.

The Merthyr Tredegar, and Abergavenny Railway runs out to the left at this place, and will, when finished, prove to be a very valuable link in the railway system, as there will be direct communication between the more westerly districts of South Wales and those of the Midland Counties. That part of the line open at present passes through GOVILAN and GILWERNB to BRYNMAWR. The

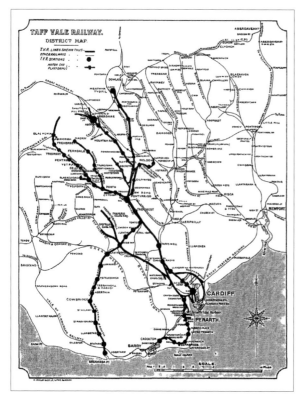

The Taff Vale Railway

This is one of the oldest and best known railways of South Wales. Its primary function was to connect the many coalfields and foundries in the valleys with the docks at Cardiff. Started in 1836 the main section between Merthyr and Cardiff was completed in 1841. The TVR operated as an independent railway until 1922 when it became a part of the GWR. It was a busy line and at its peak two trains passed through Pontypridd every minute – *see page 88*. The railway company held a virtual monopoly over the Rhondda's mine and foundry owners until the construction of the Barry Railway in the 1880s. The Taff Vale line is still in use.

Left: The gentle curve of the Cefn Coed Viaduct, just to the north of Merthyr Tydfil. The third longest viaduct in Wales, it was built in 1866 to carry the Brecon and Merthyr railway over the River Taff at Pontycapel. *(Perceval)*

rest of the journey through Tredegar to Merthyr is performed by coach, which runs once a day each way, in connection with one of the trains.

LLANFIHANGEL and PANDY stations.

PONTRILAS.
Telegraph station at Hereford, 10¾ miles.
MONEY ORDER OFFICE at Hereford.

ST. DEVERAUX and TRAM INN stations being passed, we shortly arrive at Hereford, particulars of which will be found on page xxx.

[Branch from Cardiff on the Taff Vale to Merthyr and Brecon]

TAFF VALE

Cardiff to Aberdare and Merthyr.

LLANDAFF.
POPULATION, 6,585.
Telegraph station at Cardiff, 3½ miles.
HOTEL – Railway.
MONEY ORDER OFFICE at Cardiff.

LLANDAFF, a small decayed village, but the seat of a diocese, founded in the 5th century, having a half ruined *Cathedral*, 270 feet long, chiefly in the early English style. The south door is Norman. Some old monuments are seen – one being ascribed to Dubritias, the first bishop.

From Llandaff, in the course of about half an hour, we are hurried past the stations of WALNUT TREE Junction, TREFOREST, and NEWBRIDGE, the junction of the Rhondda Valley line, via PORTH to YSTRAD and TREHERBERT. ABERDARE BRANCH.

MOUNTAIN ASH and TREAMAN stations.

ABERDARE.
POPULATION, 32,299.
A telegraph station.
HOTELS – Boot and railway.
MARKET DAY – Saturday.
FAIRS – April 1st and 16th, November 13th.

Pontypridd

At one time Pontypridd boasted of having the longest station platform in the world. The photograph *above* shows fodder being collected for the pit ponies during the 1910 coal strike. *(LoC) Below:* Postcard image of the 1911 train crash near Pontypridd. Eleven people were killed in a collision between a passenger train and a coal train on the Taff Vale line. *(CMcC)*

The scenery of the vale of Cynon here is charming. A little beyond there is a junction with the Vale of Neath Railway to Merthyr.

Taff Vale Main Line continued.

QUAKER'S YARD and TROEDYRHIEW stations.

MERTHYR.
POPULATION, 83,875.
A telegraph station.
HOTELS – Castle, Bush.
MARKET DAYS – Wednesday and Saturday.
BANKERS – Wilkins and Co.; Branch of West of England and South Wales District Banking Company.

MERTHYR TYDVIL is a parliamentary borough, the great mining town, in South Wales, 21 miles from Cardiff, with which there is a railway communication by a branch out of the South Wales line. It stands up the Taff, among the rugged and barren-looking hills in the north-east corner of Glamorganshire, the richest county in Wales for mineral wealth. About a century ago the first iron works were established here, since which the extension has been amazingly rapid. Blast furnaces, forges, and rolling mills are scattered on all sides. Each iron furnace is about 55 feet high, containing 5,000 cubic feet; and capable of smelting 100 tons of pig-iron weekly, as there are upwards of 50, the annual quantity of metal may

Below: Early view of a mine in the Rhondda Valley. The railways were a vital link.

Dowlais Ironworks and Steelworks

Bradshaw writes at some length about the foundry at Dowlais. 'Visitors should see the furnaces by night when the red glare of the flames produces an uncommonly striking effect.' Founded in 1759, from the mid-nineteeth century it was run by Lady Charlotte Guest and Edward Divett following the death of Thomas Guest. The pair revived the company through the adoption of the Bessemer process for steel production. Lady Guest died in 1895. Her daughter-in-law's name is commemorated in works loco No.33, *Lady Cornelia*. The main works survived until the 1930s, ceasing production at Dowlais in 1936. *(CMcC)*

be tolerably estimated; but great as the supply may seem, it is scarcely equal to the demand created for it by railways. The largest works are those belonging to Lady Guest and Messers. Crawshay, where 3,000 to 5,000 hands are employed. At Guest's Dowlais works there are 18 or 20 blast furnaces, besides many furnaces for puddling, balling, and refining; and 1,000 tons of coal a day are consumed.

Visitors should see the furnaces by night when the red glare of the flames produces an uncommonly striking effect. Indeed, the town is best visited at that time, for by day it will be found dirty, and irregularly built, without order or management, decent roads or footpaths, no supply of water, and no public building of the least note, except Barracks, and a vast Poor-House, lately finished, in the shape of a cross, on heaps of the rubbish accumulated from the pits and works. Cholera and fever are, of course, at home here, in scenes which would shock even the most 'eminent defender of the filth,' and which imperatively demand that their Lady owner should become one of 'the Nightingale sisterhood' for brief space of time. Out of 695 couples married in 1845, 1,016 persons signed with marks, one great secret of which social drawback is the unexampled rapidity with which the town has sprung up; but we hope that proper measures will be taken henceforth by those who draw enormous wealth from working these works, to improve the condition of the people. Coal and iron are found together in this part of Wales, the coal being worked mostly by levels, in beds 2 to 3 feet thick. Besides the large and small works in and about Merthyr, there are those at Aberdare (a growing rival to Merthyr), Herwain, Pentwain, Blaenavon, Brynmawr, Nantyglo, Ebbew (*w* as *oo*) Vale, Beaufort, Tredegar, Rhimney, Sirhowy, &c., nearly all seated at the head of the valleys, and many of them being in the neighbouring county of Monmouth, which, though reckoned part of England, is essentially Welsh in its minerals, scenery, and people. Railways and canals now traverse these valleys to the sea.

Merthyr Tydvil, as well as its church, derives its name, signifying the Martyr Tydvil, from St. Tudfyl, the daughter of Brysham (a Welsh chief) who was put to death for her religion in the early ages of the British church. Many such confessors are commemorated in the designation bestowed on parishes in Wales.

In the neighbourhood are the following objects of notice. The Taff may be ascended to Quaker's Yard and Newbridge, where there are large metal works, and a bridge, called Pont-y-Prid in Welsh, remarkable as the production of a self-taught local architect, named Edwards, who built it in 1751. It is a single arch, with a rise of one-fourth of the span, which is 140 feet, yet it is only 2½feet thick in the crown. Once and twice it fell when completed, but the third time the builder was successful, experience having taught him to diminidh the strain from its own weight, by boring three large holes on each side near the piers. Following the Neath rail, you come to Pont-neath-Vaughan, at the head of the fine Vale of Neath, within a few miles of which are the Hcfcstc, Purthin, and its branches, which are 40 to 70 or 80 feet down. One on the Mellte is particularly worth notice, as it flows for half-a-mile through a limestone cave, and then re-appears just before

BRITISH COAL STRIKE - LLWYNPIA, SOUTH WALES, A COLLIERY VILLAGE

The coalfields of South Wales fuelled Britain's industrial might throughout the nineteenth century and continued in production well into the twentieth. *Above:* Miners at a Monmouthshire colliery. *(CMcC) Left:* Mining communities were built cheek by jowel with the mines. (LoC)

The Guardian of the Valleys – this man of steel stands almost 70 feet tall. Created by artist Sebastien Boyesen, it commemorates the fiftieth anniversary of the 1960 mining disaster at Six Bells which claimed the lives of forty-five men. *(Alyson Tippings, Blaenau Gwent County Borough Council)*

it sweeps down a fall of 40 feet, with so clean a curve that people have actually taken shelter from the rain under it, on a narrow ledge in the face of the rock. The smaller spouts are called Sewbs (*w* as *oo*). These are all in Brecknockshire; but there is one of 90 feet at merlin court, half-way down the Vale of Neath; and to the right of this an ancient Roman way, called Sarn Helen, or via Julia Montana, may yet be traced. It went from an important Roman station. The direct road from Merthyr to Brecon is through a lofty pass, called Glyn Tarrell, having the Brecnockshire Beacons, 2,862 feet high on one side, and Mount Cafellente, 2,394 feet high, on the other. A considerable portion of this route has been laid with rails, and with the exception of a small portion from Merthyr to Dowlais, which is at present performed by coach, is in operation.

The route lies through DOWLAIS, DOLYGAER, TALYBONT, and TALLYLLYN to

BRECON.

Telegraph station at Abergavenny, 21 miles.

HOTELS – The Castle; Swan.

MARKET DAYS – Wednesdays and Saturdays.

FAIRS – First Wednesday in March, July 5, September 9, November 16; also in March and November 16, for hiring.

RACES in September.

This place is situated in the midst of very beautiful mountain scenery, has a population of 5,673, returning one member to parliament. It is 20 miles from Abergavenny, and communicable by coach every day. The principle buildings consist of three churches, County Hall, and Market House, very handsome new Assize Courts, built in 1843, Barracks, Theatre, Infirmary, a bridge of seven arches over the USK, from which is a fine view; there are also an Independent Training College and Grammar School at which Jones, the county historian, was educated.

Here are the remains of an old castle, consisting of the 'Ely Tower', so called from Dr. Morton, Bishop of Ely, who was a prisoner at the instance of Richard III, and as the scene of the conference between the Bishop and the Duke of Buckingham. Newmarch, a Norman baron, was the founder of the castle. Hugh Price, the founder of Jesus College, at Oxford, was born here; and Shakespeare's Fluellen, or Sir David Gow lived in the neighbourhood. He was knighted at Agincourt by Henry V, when at the point of death, having sacrificed his own life to save the king's. Another native of the Brecon was Mrs. Siddons. The 'Shoulder of Mutton' Inn is pointed out as the place of her nativity. It stands in a romantic part of the Usk, by the banks of which beautiful walks are laid out. To the north of it (22 miles by the lower and 17 by the upper road) is Builth. There are good sulphur springs in this quarter, viz: Park Wells, Llanwrtyd Wells, Llandrindod Wells, &c. Making the descent of the Usk you come to Crickhowell, where there is good angling, and (what is rare in the county) a spire church.

Brunel's broad gauge

The broad gauge was Brunel's most glorious failure. In principle the the wider gauge of just over 7 feet made a lot of sense, but the problem came when Brunel's burgeoning GWR network and connected lines met up with the standard gauge lines descending fromt the north of England. *Left:* The *Fire Fly* gave its name to a class of 2-2-2 locos designed by Gooch in the early 1840s.

The conflict between the competing gauges came to a head where they met. At Gloucester all passengers, goods, and even horses, had to be transferred from one train to another. These images were published by *The Illustrated London News* at the height of the 'Battle of the Gauges'. The turmoil might have been exaggerated for political effect, but clearly a solution was needed and in 1846 the Gauge Commission found in favour of the narrower 'standard' gauge.

The findings of the Gauge Commission didn't bring the broad gauge to an immediate end, but it had been its death warrant. Some broad gauge lines continued to be constructed where they linked with existing broad gauge lines. Elsewhere many lines were laid as mixed gauge with a third rail, but full conversion was inevitable.

Right: This broad gauge replica, the *Iron Duke,* is displayed at the Gloucestershire Worcestershire Railway at Toddington, Gloucestershire. *Below:* Broad gauge graveyard at Swindon where the locos await scrapping following the final conversion of the mainline in 1892. *Bottom:* The South Wales line was converted in stages in 1872. This is the scene at Grange Court.

Michael Portillo with the editor of Amberley's Bradshaw's Guides, John Christopher, at Paddington Station in 2012 during filming for the *Great British Railway Journeys* television series.

Bradshaw's Guides from Amberley Publishing

Acknowledgements

I would like to acknowledge and thank the many individuals and organisations who have contributed to the production of this book. Unless otherwise stated all new photography is by the author. Additional images have come from a number of sources and I am grateful to the following: The US Library of Congress *(LoC)*, Campbell McCutcheon *(CMcC)*, the Image Archive, Wendy Harris, the National Archives, Frank Whittle, Derek Webb, the British Library, Andrew Hulme, Perceval, and Alyson Tippings of Blaenau Gwent County Borough Council. Apologies to anyone left out unknowingly and any such errors brought to my attention will be corrected in subsequent editions. Thanks also to Eleri Pipien at Amberley for additional picture research. *JC*